ONENESS

—— *of* ——

BEING AND MANIFESTATION

Beyond the Dream: The Anchor Point

FRANK SCOTT AND NISA MONTIE

BALBOA.
PRESS

A DIVISION OF HAY HOUSE

Balboa Press books may be ordered through booksellers or by contacting:

Balboa Press
A Division of Hay House
1663 Liberty Drive
Bloomington, IN 47403
www.balboapress.com
1 (877) 407-4847

Because of the dynamic nature of the Internet, any web addresses or links contained in this book may have changed since publication and may no longer be valid. The views expressed in this work are solely those of the author and do not necessarily reflect the views of the publisher, and the publisher hereby disclaims any responsibility for them.

The author of this book does not dispense medical advice or prescribe the use of any technique as a form of treatment for physical, emotional, or medical problems without the advice of a physician, either directly or indirectly. The intent of the author is only to offer information of a general nature to help you in your quest for emotional and spiritual well-being. In the event you use any of the information in this book for yourself, which is your constitutional right, the author and the publisher assume no responsibility for your actions.

Print information available on the last page.

ISBN: 978-1-9822-1361-9 (sc)
ISBN: 978-1-9822-1360-2 (hc)
ISBN: 978-1-9822-1364-0 (e)

Library of Congress Control Number: 2018911776

Balboa Press rev. date: 10/04/2018

One Family

We are nature's children,
Beings infinite and bright,
Dancing through this life for joy
with laughter, love, and light.
Loving our Creator, listening within,
Serving all life's unity while
the Earth does spin.
One family of Great Spirit
bringing harmony,
Ringing Beauty from the Soul,
God's gift to you and me,
'Neath the shade of eternity's Tree—
God's gift to let us see.

Contents

Preface

Throughout *the Journey of Life*, every entity will complete a number of stages, each a step closer to understanding and experiencing the significance of the *Oneness of Being and of Manifestation*, that is, the Presence of God in one's Self, and the Illumination expressing through active participation that which exhibits those attributes—Unity.

And beyond that, through the heart, the seeker of the Truth—that God does what He Wills and Pleases—shall, through the various degrees of purification, and nearness, be given the experiences *that Reveal the Beauty of the Adored One*.

The reader will be guided through this understanding in accordance with what was ascribed and destined, and fate has sealed.

Leaves on the Tree

Each leaf's a virtue
Clearly expressed
Blowing past the Soul
As each Being manifests.

Unity's Tree alights
Where Love is whispering
The perfect Garden's secret
Beneath the Sun's delight.

He Wishes and Wills—
Steers every flight
Of wayward spirits seeking
Ways around His Might.

Nearer to Him they're drawn
Like sap from root to leaf-vein,
For who can escape the trap?
Ecstasy can't be explained.

Without His Love they crumple
Like leaves thirsting for storms
'Til clouds shadow the sky,
Colors burst arching forms.

FRANK SCOTT AND NISA MONTIE

This Oneness addresses the *principle of singleness* and *integration of the Soul, the Spirit, the Mind, and the Heart*. There is thus *unanimity*, and by default *unity* (the Lesser Covenant). It is an agreement (the Greater Covenant) reflective of a solidarity as *servants of God*, and each other. The Soul is thus the depository of God's Image and Trust through which His *Beauty* is Revealed. This Charge and Faith of God, His Beauty, which at its Root attracts and benefits His creatures, blessing them by bringing forth the splendor and magnificence of a Divine Potential that already existed from the beginning that has no beginning, and will continue to the end that has no end.

God's Will and Faith in His Creation becomes the Spirit animating His Divine Plan, and through the *Instrument of Faith*, His Assurance and Constancy, the traveling entity, in the realm of time, becomes cognizant of his or her True Self and station. This Self in all entities is in a state, by Divine Decree, of absolute oneness and unity with the All.

It is the connection to the entity's Higher Self that, when lost, gives birth to an egoic self-love imprisoning and entrapping him or her in worlds of time—away from the Beloved of all the worlds. It is this descent and separation that is referred to as Hell.

What all travelers need to understand is what lies behind the state of Oneness and Unity in practical terms. It is necessary always to be cognizant of the Oneness and Unity that pervades creation to understand how this Oneness and Unity works, and, ultimately, how it is to be experienced. We can recognize its tell-tale patterns through the quality of our lives, both individually and collectively, over the short or long term. The state of Oneness is expressive of the one Life and Intelligence throughout, and its Unity, as One Organism—the correlation and communication of all its *Spiritual* components originating within the imperceptible fields of activity of the mineral, plant, and animal kingdoms, as well as from the fifth-dimensional level of the Soul-possessing entities that act as forces engaged throughout the Simulator and Trainer.

Life and Intelligence is then viewed as the outer-most sphere of interactive reciprocity, and the wellness everywhere as an ongoing film to be watched as an expression of, in the case of the traveling entities, how well each planetary system of Life and Intelligence is doing.

This system of Universal Life and Intelligence is an intelligent design able to execute micro-adjustments at all times, changes that reflect a statistical conservation, and efficiency, of itself anywhere and at any time. All actions and activities are effectively carrying consequences not always understood or dealt with correctly, accruing thus major alterations and adjustments that appear as disordered and tumultuous at the surface, as well as uncooperative and against the grain of the desires and interests of one or more of the visiting travelers.

It is therefore for humanity's best interest to begin to understand, and cooperate with, all of the pre-existing collective of systems of Life and Intelligence and see through it, at its core, the Oneness and Unity reigning, expressing the Will and Pleasure of its Creator.

When we do not, the following consequences occur that serve as an example…. What do weapons, cigarettes, liquor, pharmaceuticals, addictions, fertilizers, polluted waters, plastics, dams, nuclear power plants, industrial fumes, abortions, criminal actions, pornography, floods, mud slides. earthquakes, volcanic eruptions, cyclones, cross-contaminants, wars, and mobile phones, to name a few, have in common? They are all destructive at some level and moment in time.

Often, we, as traveling entities, visitors that reside in a hotel named Earth, are so disconnected that we cannot help ourselves, and therefore bring disruptive actions that sever the life and intelligence of everything, including ourselves. Why is our denial still prevalent in one way or another, today?

Some entities wake up from their lethargy, blankness of Spirit, and apathy to come to their senses. At some level of their conscious-awareness there is an indication that the Universe's Life and Intelligence has begun to be active in them. They have awakened from a nightmare of the separation from their True Selves. They seek God's Grace and Redemption, for this gives them salvation, freedom, and hope, as they are released from a life of incarceration.

Unfortunately, some who have been led astray to seek _godhood_ from within and/or from without, as they attempt to express fully their Being while pursuing their desires—without the True Guidance of the Manifestation of God's intercession or intermediation—end up distorting their Ultimate Objective, bringing thus destruction to themselves and others.

Without the _Oneness of Being and Manifestation_, what gets _revealed_ from within or from without becomes, over time, the trap that incarcerates the traveler in worlds of time. What God Reveals from within and from without is quite dissimilar to what the entity brings forth or discloses as expressions of his or her small self's desires, a depository of imperfections that will distort any and all outcomes, until the *paradise sought* becomes the nightmare that imprisons the Soul.

In trying to fulfill what the entity considers or imagines as his or her ultimate objective while in a fractional and temporal, existential experience, throughout a continual procession of lives in endless worlds of time, using all the power and abilities known and unknown, inwardly and outwardly, the traveler imprisons his or her Soul (as a point of view) in a never-ending loop of desires. This condition keeps the traveler from Remembering and Returning to his or her True Self, and instead causes the entity to remain a prisoner within the Simulator and Trainer.

What the Creator Reveals to the creature, from within and from without, offers the only way to obtain True Freedom from the unreality we think of as authentic; from the illusion the entity thinks will bring that certainty required to find contentment and happiness; from the vain imaginings the entity confuses with paradise; and from the experience of existence that leads nowhere and everywhere within the temporal worlds of creation.

What God Reveals is found in the storehouse of His Will and Pleasure, and through His Blessings the entity finds what is needed to Remember and Return to the Paradise of His Eternal Love.

This _Oneness_ of Mind and Heart _connects_ the seeker of Truth with the Eternal Realm, his or her true home. The Being of Light comes upon and experiences the Love of God, the Seventh Heaven.

Oneness

The *Mystic Knower* understands well the language of the Spirit and partakes of the many meanings found in the *Heavenly Storehouse*, while growing in nearness....

To Strive

In the beginning
Beyond all beginnings
God said,
"I love thee."

From this Love
All was born.

Can you return
The favor?

Will you?
Love.

Enlightenment

Waterfall waters streaming.
Go behind the blue-bright cascades
To where the mist eddies
In rainbows—
Cool and inviting.
Here, in the "mystic"
Paradise, behind the roar
Of waters, listen
To your heart beating.
It beats in time
With the Earth
And her waters,
With the Soul's echo
Of the inimitable Voice
In the innermost Cave
From where all life
Streams forth
And falls like stars
Spinning past galaxies.

Oneness means to have an open heart that cares, born out of a wellness reflecting inner stability and sound judgment, a solid unanimity in agreement with God's Divine Plan.

It reflects a self-effacing heart, an unassuming attitude, at once discreet and modest. In one's simplicity, the traveler is respectful and servile, submissive to the Will and Pleasure of God. Oneness is a state of *mind and heart* that lives and feels every moment to its fullness, immersed in the joy of one's Self and the company of others, in a family that is all-encompassing and complete, throughout creation and following the Divine Plan, its members as diverse as the grains of sand in all the worlds of God.

This world family emanates an ever-present sense of fulfillment, a feeling fueling the Life and Intelligence of Creation. A state of Oneness captures that process and more, traversing all domains until it reaches the Heart of the Creator, Who then reflects it back through His Love.

Back Home

Deep within the innermost
Recesses of the heart,
Beyond worlds,
In the still point
Of Knowingness,

God is waiting
With infinite patience
For each of us
To Return
Like a child
Finally come home.
Even before there is a chance
For us to knock
At the door,
The All-Knowing One
Swings it wide open
With the kindest smile
Enclosing our cold frames—
Still shivering from having been
Caught out in the storm.
Surrounding us in the warm
ocean of an embrace,
One Who already Knows
About every bump and scrape,
Every stomach ache,
Doesn't care
As long as we are back
With Him.

The *Cycle of lives* is merely a chance to move up for the Mystic Knower, a traveler who has Remembered and Returned to his or her Higher Self.

The House of the Lord

In the House of the Lord
Is a door
That opens onto everything!
Each human heart
Is a passageway
To that home.
To find our ways
Through those secret openings
Takes perseverance.
There is only one way in:
Surrender
To the way of God.
When we try to break in,
Using our ways—the hammer
Of stubborn pride,
The chisel of egoic
Resentment, envy, anger—
We only damage the walls

Of our hearts.
When we bow down
At the entrance to the Mystic Temple,
Lit with the ephemeral brilliance
Of otherworldly Light,
We become that Light
Encompassing all.
The true Temple
Has no walls.

The Absolute Oneness of Being and Manifestation is observed as a witnessed throughout Creation in the appearance of those bearing an Eternal Alliance to God—His Manifestations. Through this unique phenomenon God imposes, as an uninterrupted Source of All, on Their Stand-Alone Carrier Waves, a Historic Flow: He Who is Eternally Hidden is Seen, He Who is Eternally Far is Near. Thus a _Universe of time is Infused_, time and again, with the Elixir of Life, as Love emerges and disseminates a fresh capacity to _reflect and resonate_ anew in accordance with the _Divine Plan_ for all His creatures, so they may Remember and Return to their original state of purity, glorifying the Remembrance and Reunion with their Beloved.

The Mystic Knower sees in this _Cyclic Theme_ the opportunity to be gated out of the Simulator and Trainer, if chosen. The Oneness of Being—again whole—manifests the True Unity of Self, initiating an Eternal Life in a Realm that was always present and near. The enlightened one is finally awakened, realizing the end of the illusory dreams of self within the Pure Dream of the Beloved.

The Mystery

At the end-point of the Spiral,
In the emptiness
Before the All,
God whispers your name
Born of Love
As a Gift
Without ending.
This Gift continues,
Heart-felt, until the Day
When, Returning
From lifetimes of sorrow,
One offers up,
With outstretched hands,

The Name of Love
Back to the All-embracing One,
Then He accepts
You—and It—
With a smile that transforms
Past pain into present Joy,
Leaving no separation
Between yourself
And your Self.

The Sun

The Sun of Truth
Never stops shining.
Even in the darkest of nights
The Star's Light
Pierces every heart
Unclouded by envy, jealousy,
Or fear.
It's clear
How to strip ourselves clean
As a Spring Dawn,
Pleasantly cool,
The pink horizon blooming

Delicate as roses and bird songs
As we, every petal
Of Heart and Soul,
Open—
Listening
To the whispered of Celestial breeze,
One in the Rising Light
Of the Sun.

The purpose of the *traveler's journey* is to Remember that he or she must Return to an integration of Soul, Spirit, mind, and body, a *Oneness of Being and Manifestation* that leaves behind all expressions of a fragmented system of Life and Intelligence. That is, the traveler returns because he or she was quickened and awakened to the realization of his or her *divine origin*. His or her behavior, thoughts, feelings, and actions reflect and express that Reality, and his or her existence is the life of someone who lives in the *eternity of the Kingdom of God*.

Guided by God's Will and Pleasure, each traveler's narrative becomes a story of Remembering and Returning to this condition of Oneness of Being and Manifestation. No matter how long or short it was, or how hard and painful the experiences were, in the end, this journey was—and is—one of integration and service to all.

It is not about being right or being wrong, although it matters in the scheme of things. The main thing to Remember is the purpose of all of these experiences by asking your Self, *where are they taking me*?

By keeping in mind that each and all of these moments are valuable, we discover the pattern they form, its direction and meaning. It is not important that the shared sojourn is, or is not, one traveled in *first class*. What is central to the idea of a journey is never to lose sight of your destination, for all must return to the same origin—God.

How easy, or difficult, the journey is for ourselves and with others, is up to the Lord of all the worlds. We are being judged for our sincerity and faithfulness, for our obedience to those basic agreements we all share: The Lesser and the Greater Covenants, the rules of the Game of Life. The Divine Assayer tests us to determine to what extent we understand the Truth— that all Divine Educators represent the Creator. It is that simple. The Creator determines what each traveler needs to experience. Respect the life of others, for no one knows, in the end, what is in store for each of us.

Hidden

Under the waterfall
Lies a sign
Of Truth:
The secret Word,
Like a stone
Smoothed by centuries
Of rushing waters,
Like the Prophets' mantles
Brushing the cold hearts
Of men,
Trying to warn them
With the Fire
Hidden under water,
The flame of God's Love
Floating just under the surface
Of the purifying waves
Whose cascades
Of foam and spray
Fill the air
With rainbow-impregnated
Mist.

It is clear, to those that have eyes to see and ears to hear, that the most self-destructive action the traveler can carry out, one that brings about a disbelief in the existence of his or her Creator, is to live in denial. Such an undertaking disrupts the inward and outward connectivity, balance, and stability the traveler is required to have in order to manifest the necessary coherence (consistency and lucidity) and true functional state of the mind and heart. The danger of this state of denying life highlights the purpose and significance of Knowing and Loving God: to safeguard the traveler's Oneness of Being and Manifestation while protecting their impressionable natures, so they may remain always awake, or mindful of Self. This understanding, along with a caring and accepting attitude, during an immersion and emergence in a world of time, as a fractional and temporal, existential experience, provides for the necessary spiritual growth and nearness. When knowingness is coupled to an increased intensity of the higher energetics, infused from within, this Oneness brings into view those dimensional-states, otherwise hidden, that are necessary for each being to retain an overall affinity with the other existing components that make the material-construct the footing and beginning for the enhanced Reality experienced. This experience of enlightenment then nurses the advancement of a Divine Civilization.

Reflection

The full moon
Reflecting the light of wonder
Basks the sky
In an infinite glow.

Who can know
The Mystery, or ponder
How the Light transfers
From Sun to Moon

Save those who spy,
In space, the incredible waves
Bringing light from the Source
To the Manifested, who try

To awaken, quicken
Those sparks of Being, planetary
Lives longing to be lifted
Up through the Moon's Light.

Dive, Arise

Deep within the well
Of each human heart
Lies the water of longing
For the One Who Lives forever.
That One, hidden within
The mystery of dark waters,
Holds all Light.

Let the Light well up
From the darkness,
The Love
Bubble over the rim as we
Bend to drink
From the clear waters
Slipping over the edge
Of the crystal chalice.

This Love
Has always overflowed
With every beat and breath
Of the Heart and Soul's
Knowing.

The Sun

The Sun's light expands,
Creating morning
On a distant planet
That circles
Towards and away
From the Source,
Just as we humans
Turn,
Towards and away,
From the Unknowable Essence.

***

What if we were to surrender
To our hearts' longing
For the nurturing Mother
Of all life,
And together,
Turn our wistful faces
So that they, too,
Become lit
Along with our hearts,
With the all-encompassing

Radiance
Of Love?

Where Wonder Begins

When a star spins itself
Into a portal—a tunnel—
Of light, the bright
Radiance
Leads to eternity.
Follow His Might
To allow the unfolding
Of that which was hidden,
The blossoming
Of a delicate rose
Bowing in the Spring rains
Beneath His Infinite Mercy.

The Wind

The wind of knowledge
Blows through every heart,
Enlightening
Those who open their

Petaled selves
To the infinite
Knowingness.
Let the Mystery
Of the Breeze
Bathe the very fiber
Of the Soul
So that all that reverberates
Within
Quivers with the delight
Of a rose
Lifting its delicate petals
To receive the first
Morning dew drops
Of clear nectar
On its velvety red,
Silken surface.

Rejoice
In the ineffable
Wonder
Of innumerable
Spring mornings
Where the thirst

Is quenched
Without rain,
And the Soul is lit
Without heat—
The clear, bell-like
Blessings,
Celestial light
Emerging
Within.

One thought, rearranged from within, time and again, expands into a dot of light and more, a stream that grows into a river of light, a universe that can be seen and be held within a Soul.

Such is everything, a dot of Light when reduced, a universe when expanded and held within the space that is perceived as separating and bringing distance to bear its fruit and purpose. The entity, as a Being of Light, moves away from a Center and Anchor of an inner relationship with the Creator. The Light illumines and brings to bear its fruit, an immense universe of Knowingness and Lovingness that serves a purpose.

When all Light Beings congregate into a single moment in space, a timeless reunion of Love and

Knowingness, the Soul of Creation is now opened to be observed by all.

Close your eyes and enjoy the silence of the Oneness of Being, and breathe the breath of its Manifesting expression that bears its fruit of _Reunion with the Beloved_ of all the worlds. There is so much that was hidden and is now observable, so much that was far and is now near, as the Beauty, a dense collection of tiny particles of evanescent radiation, gather together and dance, whirling around and around to show the face of its Creator through the science and art unfolding its mysteries. There is no God but He, if ye but know it.

Full Moon

When the Moon becomes full,
Every shadow is chased away.
When the heart fills
With His Radiance,
Every thought but Him
Vanishes.
What is there to question?
Huddle next to the strong
Trunk of the oak,

Under its forgiving shadow,
When the world's
Tempestuous winds
Roar.
As night settles,
Clouds dissipate,
The Full Moon's Light
Scatters an unearthly brilliance
Through the sieving
Leaves,
Lighting the straight path
Home.

The State of Oneness of Being and Manifestation ensures affinity with everyone and everything, Spiritually and Mentally, as expressions of One Soul. We see with the same Eyes and hear with the same Ears.

Opening to the Heart

Deep within
Is the Well of Knowingness
That knows no end.
Dip into the Well,

Drink,
And be re-born.
Only you can bend
To sip
The immortal draft
From the Camphor Cup.
It takes but an instant
To leave the dry desert
Behind
And welcome
God's Gift
Of Love.

Sunshine

The light of the Sun
Illuminates all the hidden corners:
Shadowed places of the Heart,
Old sadness, "mistakes,"
Winding paths seeming to lead
Away from the Great Conjurer,
Turn bright and straight
As open plains of bliss.

Dawn colors flood
The awakened trees.
Birds sing for their mates,
Call for their little ones.
Above the ocean of Knowingness
The sky swims in waves
Of purple and orange
As every heart remembers
Bathing
In Springtime breezes
Of God's Love.

Inner Exploration

There is a tunnel
Of the Soul.
Follow it
To the Land of Light.
There is a well
Of the Heart.
Dive into it
To discover the Ocean
Of possibilities.
There is a spinning star

Of Awareness.
Let it be your eye
Of the All-seeing One:
Seeing only the Good,
Like the mother eagle
On her nest,
Caring for the helpless,
Gray and fluffy chicks.
Life is simple—
If you let it be.
Follow your heart
To the Living Tree
Of Truth.
Then sit
In its sacred shadow,
Knowing eternity exists
As the two of you
Breathe as One.

The *Oneness of Being and Manifestation*, what we see and what we don't, and what is near and what is far, is best proven and exemplified throughout the entity's sojourn on a scale of sincerity and faithfulness.

Whereas *sincerity* and earnestness embody an outlook *without any agenda*, the resulting content of a life of an entity fully expressing those virtues consists solely of the Will and Script of the Creator.

It is the All-Knowing One Who is then recognized as having chosen the entity's path and experiences that will illumine—so that he or she Remembers and Returns continuously to the Lord of all the worlds. For such entities, their mind-world constructs, as expressed in worlds of time and beyond, are filled with fractional and temporal existential experiences that all give way to the fruit and blessings inherent in a purposeful path leading back to the unity of the True Self.

And, whereas *faithfulness*, truthfulness, constancy, and authenticity stand as proof of the entity's Reality before his or her Creator, a life of confidence and Faith in the Creator fashions the individual an all-encompassing and complete assurance in His Promise, His Trust in each of us, powering one's Self-reliance and utter dependence on His Word.

The connection that for-ever exists between the creature and the Creator becomes gradually revealed, unfolding a panoramic view that transcends (trans-dimensionally) this and all sojourns that make one's journey of Remembrance and Return, until the seeker awakens, finally, one last time, as the Self proclaiming the glory of the Creator.

This connectivity assists in attenuating, mitigating, offsetting, and easing the hold of the egoic-modulation on the Stand-alone, Scalar, bi-directional and non-linear, carrier wave, within individuals and as a collective. The harmonics and attunement of Life are thus restored. The Universal Mind is tuned across its spectrum, unfolding the Love and Beauty everywhere—that which was hidden is now seen, and that which was far is now nearer.

Unseen

That which surrounds,
That which penetrates,
That which overflows,
That which permeates
Every cell,
Every molecule,
Every atom
Beyond God's Love
Is His Will.

***

We are the Trees
That fold and bend
Before Its torrential force,
The specks of dust
Blown to Kingdom Come
By the Knowing Breeze,
The echoing of His Word
Carrying creation before It.

Infused

The clear stream of Knowingness
Runs through each heart
From on High.
Dip your whole face
Into its ebullient, clarifying
Force,
Washing away
All dusty traces
Of worlds of time.
Behold—
The Light-filled world
Of His Pleasure
Surrounds your Beingness

Like a Meadow,
Redolent of Spring's
Colorful effusion of flowers,
Scent of roses and lilies
Even the wayward
Dandelion.

One of the effects, significance, purpose, and appearance of the Oneness of Being and Manifestation is best illustrated through the effect it has on the visible and the invisible as *an Anchor Point*, or connection, and all related and associative aspects bonding and uniting the Creation of God. This *unifying Theme* running throughout, the one, clear goal underlying all life, indicates and confirms the indispensable worth and usefulness of its singularity and Oneness through the fact that it benefits every entity and creature. Though we are but specks of moving dust, our existence gains merit and attention in direct proportion to the nearness of our relationship to this Foundation of stability and permanence, strength and dependability, upon which is build the soundness and reliability of *All That Is*—be it a universe, a galaxy, a planet, the life and intelligence of a species, or the individual.

Furthermore, it is through this ever-present steadiness, harmony and balance, in a state of relative equilibrium, including through the pairing phenomenon present throughout the creation, that order is brought into the many biological structures, sustaining and assisting advancement. These advances even include the financial well-being of a household, communities, nations, and, ultimately, the world commonwealth.

For as long as this _Oneness of Being and Manifestation_ remains undisturbed, ever-present, unbroken by the special interests of the few, and the desires of many, who introduce and insert the many diverse anomalies or irregularities and inconsistencies that disrupt or transform its essential Divine Design, a unity built from within as an Image, the Soul-based sensibilities, the awareness, needed to be a functional and cohesive system of Life and Intelligence, with all that becomes expressed or Manifested, the human race will witness an uninterrupted process of spiritual growth guided from the Unseen towards the Paradise of the Love of God.

Finding Certitude

The way the oak tree roots
Run deep and wide
Leaves no room for doubt

That the sap of life
Stirring root to trunk to
Leaves exists only because
Its Source underlies
Everything.
So why question
The Mystery beyond all
Mysteries when
The same soil
Of the human heart
Lies within
All hearts, and the same
Sap of life animating
One tree
Animates all trees?
The unity and oneness of life
Is like the sea—
Every wave overlapping
Every other in endless
Motion, collapsing
In the final bow
On the shores
Of consciousness,

As the spray of awareness
Creates a sparkling mist
Filling, and rising,
In the sea air.

Anchored

In the center of the Sun
Is the point of No-Return.
Find that Center
Within your Self
And let the ever-expanding
Plain of Bliss
Fill your life.
Every moment
Becomes pure—
Sparkling.
God speaks within
As your own voice
Rejoicing
In the divine blessings
Everywhere present.
There is no tomorrow—
Or yesterday.

Every moment is divine.
Find that Point
And cling to it
As a sailor to the mast
Of the ship of consciousness
Bobbing on the waves
Of endless awareness.
All glory to God
In the highest,
Bringing the Light
Of infinite suns.

Beyond

As the Sun rises and sets,
Our lives are born and die,
Leaving no trace
In the earthly sky.

Yet in the inner heaven,
Each virtue that was served
Places within the sky a star,
The heavenly sign
That God is not far.

Nearness to God means simply this—
That all God's creatures
Are slowly walking the path
Towards infinite bliss.

The thing to cling onto
Is the life-line tied to heaven.
Let go of that and you lose
All the gifts given.

The Manifestation comes each time
To free mankind of all illusions:
The dreams we see on Earth
Are made of specks of dust
That cause the Mind's confusion.

Let go in the ocean of samsara
So as not to drown.
The only thing necessary
For true Life
Lies in the region
That can't be found.

Follow the heart's guidance
To the inner Mystery

Waiting to bud.
The flower of eternity blooms
Beneath the mud.

Ten thousand years may pass
Before the Soul's awakening.
A Word from Him
Can cause the Tree Root's shaking.

Replant the Self In the soil
Newly-conditioned.
God's grace, like the sun and rain,
Will seed the Soul's re-positioning.

There is not a day
Where clouds and sun do not exchange
The patch of sky
That lies in God's pure Reign.

One thousand years, more or less,
Finds a new Tree growing.
Rest in that shade
To find your own Soul's Knowing.
If any prayer were to be offered,
Let it be this:

That God may bring me close
So I cannot be missed.

Let each Day guide One's Self
To the Infinite Source.
For God alone knows the way
On the unknowable Course.

Beyond the dream of lives
Where God is far,
Is the Infinite World
Where all hearts link
To where we are.

Lose not time in the search
For the Unsearchable One—
Heaven awaits those serving
Life—everyone.

Remember always the Key
To God's Remembering:
He waits for those who know He is
Beyond everything.

When there is no distance to travel, there is no
Journey to speak of. When there is no Journey to

speak of, there is no _boat or raft_ missed. When there is only _Oneness of Being and Manifestation_, expressed with your eternal companion, there is only Paradise. When there, there is no elsewhere.

Always

The Creator loves all His creatures, _always_. His Creation lives for as long as He exists. He is _always_ present and His Presence is His Love. _Al(l)-ways_ lead to God! The power-motive behind everything, _always_, is His Will. His Divine Plan was complete from a beginning that knows no beginning.

The Point of Origin

Inside the Tree,
Inside the sap,
Inside the molecule of sap.
Inside the atom,
Is the intention of God
Creating life.

What are we
But the manifestation

Of that intent,
Born on Earth,
In a physical body,
Living for as long as
He has intended—
Then journeying back
To our Origin,
To begin another journey
In a world of time,
Or beyond?

We can only be thankful
For the Gift of Life,
Asking always to be of service
To His Unknowable
Will.

We are given a script, and we play a role or roles during our sojourn here on Earth. _We are all where we are meant to be always_, a rendering of the many degrees of Spiritual growth, some closer and others farther, and all these scripts and ways _are designed to lead_ His creatures back to Him.

The individual entity _will integrate_ and incorporate all the attributes of a Being of Light, because he or she *was and is always* a Being of Light—subjected to illumination or enlightenment. This process of *Self-realization* begins a process of removing, by degrees, all the ignorance (the veils) that keeps the entity trapped in a loop of separation from his or her *True Self.*, The entity thus develops the ability to manage his or her energetics and subdue selfish desires. This removal or reduction of the egoic modulation reflects the increased degree of one's Heart's and Love's intensity, in turn affecting the presence of one's Soul-based awareness, as that Awareness begins to unify, from within, with the Spirit of Life and Intelligence, the Mind, and from without, with the body or vehicle during each being's sojourns of exploration and inner Self-discovery.

At some moment, in the traveler's Spiritual development, the individual entity sees with, and hears with, the Eyes and Ears that have always been there, in *a Divine Station*, reflecting an ever-present bearing or stand-point of view, that was *always* there—from the Kingdom of God.

This *transformation and transcendent process*— an otherworldly and mystical experience, an awe-inspiring and graduated state of knowingness, a knowing understood only by one's Self—continues until the True Self is fully realized, understood, and appreciated, in a moment bestowed by the Will and Pleasure of the ever-merciful Creator.

It is through this vigorous, dynamic, and vibrant translation that a lifeless entity is charged with eternal life. The temporal fades. The entity is re-created—Remembering and Returning to the Lord of all, as the mind-world constructs dissolve, and hearts are One.

Then, one takes charge with full responsibility of wherever and whatever the condition the entity finds him- or her- Self in. Complete acceptance and appreciation begin now, as God's servant-in-waiting, in order to partake of the properties given within the Plain of Limitations, the road that takes the entity to the Plane of Oneness of Being and Manifestation!

The Virtue Tree

Inside the Tree of Life
Is the running sap
Of virtues.
Each time one dip's one's
Soul-sight into the river,
The sparkling Drops
Rise like crystal dew
On the flowering

Awareness.
The Unknowable One
Lifts us,
Like leaves on His Tree,
In the virtuous Breath,
Sweeping Mind and Heart
Clean
Of the dust of desires.

Praise be to the Lord
For His Grace
From the illuminated Tree,
Shedding the cooling shade
On each of His
Humble servants,
Who find true Peace
In sharing
Kindness and compassion,
As they lean together
Against the sturdy trunk—
The Tree filling every inner Room
With His inimitable
Love.

The *process of Self-realization* is by invitation only. This and many other concepts are of great importance to the seeker of *the Truth*: that God does what He Wills and Pleases on whomever He chooses.

To Self-realize is to understand and be consciously aware of one's True Self, to be illumined continuously with the complete experience of existence, to attain to the final immersion into creation and be fulfilled with that cognition—the zenith of understanding collapsed into a single point—the Truth.

All entities have been invited Home from the moment of their creation. It is an invitation to Remember and Return to their True Selves. For some, the journey is short and sweet; for others, it is long and filled with suffering.

Spring Awakening

In the soil of Love,
Grows the Tree,
Infused with Grace,
Leaves lifted by His breath,
That anoints each creature
With eternity.

Filling the space,
Within and without,
Leaves whisper,
Branches delineate
Space collapsed into time,
Roots sink deep
In the timeless Garden.
Rejoice.

Long-lasting

Within the heart of every human
Is a star of power—
The Flowering of His Cause,
Mirror of His Grace.
Let it spin and shine,
The divine pleasure
Within the inner Tree,
The true freedom
Allowing each entity to be
The True Self of the One,
The invincible nothingness,
No-ego-ness,
Providing each sentient

Being with the overwhelming
Gratitude, the attitude
Of gratefulness
For the gift of everlasting
Life
In His Presence,
The ultimate present
Of existence.

Steadfast

The way a river
Bends around a boulder
In its path,
Or an eagle banks
In a storm
To reach its windy nest,
Or our hearts open
To the unburning fire—
Sacrificing self
To Self—
Must continue,
Past knowing

Where the pathless Path
Will lead.

Sometimes, before dawn,
A small Whisper comes,
Saying,
"Wake up. Write. Live
A moment in my Presence."
I obey—moth to flame—
Rising and washing
The sleep from my eyes,
Then taking pen and paper
In hand to wait,
Heart upturned
Like a morning rose, listening
For the words that let me know
He is near.

Transmutation
and Faith

Spiritual transformation is the objective behind the _Oneness of Being and Manifestation_ during the traveler's immersion in the shores of consciousness in a world of time. We Remember and Return to that _Original State_ of purity of intent, reflecting that condition in everyday life, and becoming luminous beings and servants of God.

Such is the effect of the Word of God on any traveling entity, through the Soul's modulation on the stand-alone, scalar, bi-directional and non-linear, carrier wave. As we progress Spiritually, our states of Knowingness and Lovingness increase, reflecting the intensity of God's Love within each of us. It is this Love that binds and holds the creature to his or her Creator, each other, and everything.

Through the _Spirit of Faith_, an instrument acting on the relevant imperceptible fields of activity through the Heart, the traveling entity acquires _the confidence_ to work and live within the realms of matter (the third-dimensional state), mind (the fourth-dimensional state), and the Spirit itself (the fifth-dimensional state).

As the Heart of the traveler brings the Higher Self's integration and participation to bear its presence upon the arena of life, the traveler's confidence increases. It is an upward, ever-embracing process that opens up, and gives access to, the entity's true identity and gifts, resulting in contributions to the whole that advance a divine civilization.

The Spirit of Faith allows the traveler to complete his or her Return, and be his or her True Self. Through each of the steps integrating the Being of Life and Intelligence with its mission, the entity acts in obedience to the Law (the sixth-dimensional state of the Heart), becomes righteous and compassionate (the seventh-dimensional state of the Heart), lives within the Love of God (the eight-dimensional state of the Heart), and surrenders his or her will to the Will and Pleasure of God (the ninth-dimensional state of the Heart), to become Self-realized (the tenth-dimensional state and above)—as an observer and participant in the fractional and temporal, existential experience.

Transformation

As the Tree spreads its branches,
God's Words rain down—
On prairies, mountains, seas, peoples,
Animals, plants, even minerals
Magically transformed
Into Paradise
Rooted in Wisdom.

Supplication to God

O Great Mystery,
Unknowable Essence,
Unknown One:
We ask Thee,
Entreat thy present favor,
To enlighten us
With Thy wisdom,
As the Tree is illumined
With the rays
Of the rising sun.

Grant us Thy protection
In these time of troubles,
And Thy blessings
To know right action
When the path is choked
With weeds,
As well as flowers.

Grant us Thy favor
To know when to speak
And when to be silent,
When to act
And when to remain still,
And when to let go
Any idea of anything—
So Thy Will may be done.

Through these four ways the traveler becomes the Mystic Knower, and witnesses the Glory of God (Baha'u'llah): guided by Moses, the Law Giver, the way of obedience, fraught with conflict at first; then, illumined by the way of compassion and righteousness, the Seeker now reflects on the world of time, the wisdom of the Buddha; and moves on to learn to live within the precinct of the Love of God, the way of the

Anointed One, the Christ; and finally, the seeker of the Truth learns about surrendering to the Will and Pleasure of the Creator, the way of Muhammad, the Apostle of God.

Each step, a process by degrees, takes the Seeker in a Journey upon the shores of consciousness, a fractional and temporal, existential experience that is either bringing the traveler closer to, or farther, from the goal—Reunion with the Beloved of all the worlds.

The Transfer

Thy Radiance illumines
As the Sun
The whole Earth,
Thy dawning Smile,
Filling eternity
Like lightning
Slicing a Tree without
Annihilating.

Me
In the Heart to heart
Transfer.
I am all Light—Spirit,

All bright—no spark,
Relieved from dark mortality's
Strictures

Despite looking outwards at the play
Whilst the unburning Flame
Fills the Soul's clear mirror
Entirely.

Below the Surface

Underneath the seeming endless
Waves of the Divine Ocean
Lies the Stillness
Of All-Knowing,
The Point of Return,
Glittering Mirror
Reflecting it-Self
In the Heart's Wonder.

Without Wonder,
The Spirit tosses
From sea-womb to rough and craggy
Shore, left to dry
Like sea-lettuce

Browning in the sun,
Half-covered
In grainy sand.

Let the wonder at God's Gift
Of Existence grow,
Immovable, towering
Mountains
Thrust up from His Faith
In us, spreading in a delicate range
Of orange and pink
Sun-rise ribbons
Across the New Morning's
Sky.

Everywhere
He listens for the signs
Of our Soul's shaking
In the breeze of Delight,
Awakening from the dream
Of separation as we stretch out

Our arms like babes embracing
The Mystery and Love
Ringing a thousand, Clear-sounding

Bells
Of His
Unmistakable
Presence.

As energy is converted into matter, and vis a vis, matter is converted back into energy at the square root of the speed of light within the Simulator and Trainer, everything is drawn and erased so fast that entities do not become aware that they are in a _dream within a Dream_. More importantly, they miss the fact that they live within a Trainer designed to manifest the _traveler's innermost states_ of connection or disconnection with their Soul-based states of Awareness, as well as their dimensional capacity to participate in the manifestation of a _heaven-like or hell-like state of affairs_ in the world of time we are all sharing.

We eat to produce the energy that gets converted into the mass we observe and live with, frame after frame, back and forth, drawn and erased so rapidly, from a wave to a particle, as a _stand-alone, bidirectional and nonlinear, uninterrupted carrier wave_, a process that allows the traveler to stay within the Dream, explore and discover the many things that will lead him or her back to his or her True Self, while assisting, or not, a never-ending and divine civilization.

Peace

Beyond the pain
Of freedom and incarceration
Is the Oneness of Life
Eternal.
How to find it?
Simply look within
The Heart of hearts
To where the All-Knowing One
Dwells.
Here, in the peace
Of His Loving-Kindness,
Flowing like a breeze
Lightly-rippling
The heart's river—
The blood of Faith—
The stillness evokes
The New Dawn
Of awareness.

Everything in life
Rejoices, knowing
That His Presence

Animates every-One.
We pray to God,
That through His Glory,
We may find our ways back
To the healing Center
Of infinitude.

Life

Deep within the Sun's Center
Is Life It-Self:
The swirling mass of bright
Air—on fire.
What would Life be
Without the Fire
Of His Love,
Burning illusion
Like bright party paper?
What are our Hearts
Made of except
The shining examples
Of Peace—the Rivers
Of Contentment
Flowing into the Sea

Of Divine Certitude?

Life it-Self has neither end
Nor beginning:
How can an Ocean
Squeeze its mighty form
Into a drop?
Pick any point in the universe
And you will find
That it can be collapsed
Into any other point.
Each Being's supposed
"Uniqueness" is just a turning
Of the Crystal Source,
The Sun lighting up
A different point of view
On the surface
Of Life's Beauty.

Find that point—that portal—
That is You,
Divine within.
The Journey is endlessly inviting
Like a cascade

Of clear water
Rising
And descending
Towards the infinite Unknown
In the clear, crystal cave
Of the Heart's wonder.

The traveling entity is continuously immersed in the *dream within a Dream*, an expression of his or her own state of Spiritual (at the vacuum level) development, enveloped in a seeming struggle of wills, as creature and Creator, until the creature realizes the futility of its egoic strivings, and the Truth of it all—that God, the Great Mystery, the Transcendent, the Unknowable Essence, is, and was always, in control—He does what He Wills and Pleases on whomever He chooses.

And when the traveler Awakens some day, in the Day of God, the complete understanding of the *Journey of Separation and Return*, death and resurrection, will be understood.

The Given Path

Care-free as we seem to be
Without God's strictures,
We are lost

To our-Selves when
The Infinite One's Holy
Ways are forgotten.

The only answer is Return
To the True Home, the only
One nesting in the Heart
Of the Universe, hidden
Within each Being's
Innermost, special, secret
Cave of the heart
Where always
Waits the Unknown Great Being's
Demand: Live in obedience
To My Commands.

If a ship Captain
Were to let his trawler
Yawl all over the ocean,
Until finally hitting
Smack against a stray wave
Broadside—the Wrong
Direction—guess what follows?
The ship leans so off

Center that
It capsizes
Into the cold emptiness—
All hands lost.

Leaving behind mistakes, trips
That founder on shores
Of egoic `fancies',
We cleave (by God's Grace)
To Joy, find lit
The path of Radiance—
See His Face.

Beyond Knowing

Beyond the light of the Sun
Is another Sun—brighter
Than the rest—lightning hearts
The Brilliant Truth
Obliterates
The darkest nest.

Illuminating the path of right,
Burning forever
With the Self's Light,

FRANK SCOTT AND NISA MONTIE

The Truth Incarnate
Extends a hand.
Manifesting rays
To lift us to His Land,

So we may breathe,
Absorb virtues apace,
Steeped in the fragrance
Of God's Mercy and Grace.

Without this Sun
We're imprisoned, condemned,
Inside wall of passion
For the fleeting—
Only His Love amends.

Infinite Glory can't be seen—
We're blinded by the Light,
So we close our eyes and bow
To the Glory
Beyond Sight.

The traveling entity is being led to a higher degree of Knowingness and Lovingness through four ways or processes: the way of the Law (obedience), the way of

Detachment and Contemplation, (righteousness and compassion), the way of Love (attraction), and the way of Understanding (surrendering to the Will and Pleasure of the Creator). As we purify our hearts, the depository of our intentions, and cleanse our minds of all egoic thoughts that rob us of our _True Direction_, we are aligned with the Divine Design and objective of Remembering and Returning to our True Selves. This objective, or _Anchor Point_, may be viewed as a point of reference that indicates whether each traveler is either moving to worlds of time that assist in his or her advancement (moving closer to the Higher Self) towards his or her liberation from the Simulator and Trainer, or is being further immersed in worlds of time deemed necessary for that entity to realize that his or her egoically-based way and modulation _does not work_!

The traveler is constantly expressing (manifesting the qualities and properties of) either his or her freedom from, or further incarceration in, the Simulator and Trainer: towards the Higher Self (Remembering and Returning), or away from his or her True Self. This _bidirectional communication_ is composed of none other than the creature's Love intended for God, and the Creator's Love designed for His creature.

If the imposition of signals on the entity's stand-alone carrier wave (the entity's state of being within the Simulator), was initiated at the Soul-based state of Awareness (the Holy Spirit), its _transmission and translation_ (the energy/matter bi-directional flux), generates (as a reflection) an outward state of perfections, such as well-being and wisdom, and other attributes of the Kingdom of God. If, on the other hand, imperfections are predominant in the life of the entity, such as ignorance or the lack of management of one's passions, then we can conclude that the modulations on that individual's carrier wave (as impositions of information) are egoically-based, that is, lacking the contribution of the Grace of God (Soul-based modulation).

Foundations

When the wave enters the field of consciousness,
All sorts of miracles ensue:
The babe is born
From a burgeoning egg.

The sapling tree
Begins its journey
From seed
To slender trunk and leafy branches.

The human mind begins to buzz
With thoughts of eternity,
Coalitions of sense-perceptions
Divinely translated.

Soul and Spirit
Become apparent
As rippling reflections
On the surface of the wave,

Until we bow down
Before the miracle of existence—
Humble servants,
Wavelets on the wave.

Eternal Love

When the wave enters the human heart,
The Love of God steals in,
Quietly. Secretly.

In just such a way the Flicker woodpecker,
Claws gripping the side of the palm tree
Next to the small, perfectly round
Entrance to its home,

Calls once
Its wild-throated cry for its mate,
Then suddenly disappears through
The portal to alight (we assume)
Within the nest
With the Beloved.

Two birds are united,
Within the hallowed
Tree.

When God's Faith (Divine Information dispensed by His Manifestations) is absent, as the Source of Self-reliance, the heart, now empty, fills itself with other bits and pieces of information that give and bring alternate sources of self-assurance.

Armed with this conviction and faith in the realms of the material, mental, and even the imperceptible field of life's potential, the traveler is poised and perched on a third-, fourth-, or even a fifth- dimensional story that limits the greater and more far-reaching One from delivering the ultimate freedom beyond the Simulator and Trainer. The traveler clings to the wrong rope—resources that twist him or her in the air, leading to loops entwining his or her attention with the things that matter little for True Enlightenment and Self-realization; They distract the seeker from the level that offers each Light Being, upon the confluence of the *Four Spiritual Ways*, the recognition and appreciation of every Sojourn's objective of True Remembrance and Return to one's True Self.

The ways of obedience, righteousness and compassion, love and forgiveness, and surrender and submission, that lead to the Glory of God and Self, are simply dismissed and forgotten, while being replaced by an ardent desire to connect to these lesser paths that bond the traveling entity to a physical universe within the Simulator and Trainer, a large and unrecognizable prison enticing and luring, like everything else, while keeping the True Search from commencing.

Yet, despite this apparent misdirection, in the end, any and all of these immersions in the ocean of consciousness serve a purpose, regardless of how such diversions prolong the Sojourn of Remembrance and Return and lengthen the time before each entity may fully experience the Beloved of all the worlds.

That Love

The thing that makes life tick,
The thing that makes us move
From creatures of dust

To Beings of Light,
Is the Infinite Source:
The Mystery of Mysteries
Shining Love
Like a Beacon
To draw us all back
To our Selves.

The Welcoming

Like the volcano's lava
Pouring red-hot
From the center of the Earth,
Thy Love annihilates everything
In its path.
Trees are burnt to a blackened crisp.
Ducks landing on a pond
Find it has turned to steam,
Fled to four thousand miles away.
Humans, fearing Thy Power,
Run through what's left
Of the grass, then
From a distance—turn

To watch the mountain,
Dissolved into rivers of fire.
What's left when God's Messenger
Lights a fire
In each heart?

The Infinite Flow

The way a River flows downhill,
The way a Mountain grows
To the sky,
The way a Heart
Longs for God—
This is the way Life moves:
An inexorable necessity.
Like wave upon waves,
We fling our Selves
On the shore of His Mercy,
Begging God
Standing within the Tree
Of His perfect Self,
To bring us nearer.
There is no limit to how near
He may draw us in—

As a pink rose in full bloom
In the glowing First Light,
Suns shimmering in the scattered
Dew drops on its velvet-petalled
Surface, attracts
Effortlessly
The iridescent, invisible-winged
Hummingbird
To deep within its pulsing,
Nectar-filled Center.
Just so, God takes His Breath
And blows away the tears
Of separation
Off His offspring, whispering
Words of Love,
Drawing, and re-drawing
The Soul's Longing
To be imprinted
With His gifts,
As a Crystal
Swaying and turning
In the breeze
On the Cord of His Love

Shines tiny rainbows
Here and here
On leaves and grass and walls
To show that nothing solid
Exists—only light
Focused from Love
Throughout Infinity.

Following Faith

Along the river banks
Grow flowers
Of different colors.
Each of these flowers
Represents a different virtue.
All of them together equal
The Glory of God.
The River is the Holy Spirit
Running throughout—and beyond—
Time, knitting together
All the lives
Into One Life on the planet.
This One Life
Is the Essence of Humanity,

The Spirit of Life
Endowed with the Grace of God.
Each time each of us prays,
This Spirit of Life shakes
And reverberates
With His Will, as a Tree
Shakes and reverberates
In the wind and rain
Of a Great Storm.

We are here on Earth
To listen with all
Our hearts and Soul
To God whispering...
Through the waves
Of the River, the Wind's
Roaring Voice, the steady
Beat of rain
Upon the bending, green
Leaves of the Tree.

His Love echoes
Along the river bank,
Embraces each different—colored

Flower,

And unites all

Through the Spirit

Of Faith,

As We Witness our own

Creation

In each tiny drop

Of falling water.

The *prodigal son or daughter* has Returned. The end and the beginning now overlap and give birth to a new Eternal Realm—away from the fractional and temporal, existential experiences. In Remembering his or her True Self, the entity's continuing experience with the Beloved has become a conscious state of Being.

In practical terms, having the capacity to perceive and feel, with the correct attitude and intent derived from the Station of the Manifestation of God, with one's *Being in a State of Oneness and Manifestation*, is akin to Knowing what needs to be known, always. In such a state, our Being is able to superpose the beauty and perfections of the Eternal Realm upon the imperfections and anomalies of this plane of existence of Earth. These changes are significant in that they reflect God's Will and Pleasure—done on Earth, as it is done in Heaven.

As each and all travelers, generation after generation, serve the Divine Plan as servants who see, hear, speak, and act in accordance with His Will and Pleasure, these heaps of moving dust become the resplendent abode, a rose planted in the garden of each of His creatures' hearts, _our gift to the Stealer of Hearts_.

This process of transformation and Self-realization has _One Beginning_, one Point of Entry that brings the experience of being gated-in, and piped, connected to the Soul-based state of pure awareness and the Spirit of Life and Intelligence of the universe, and Creation as a whole; while each one of us, as travelers in the Journey of exploration and Self-discovery, experiences the Resurrection and Awakening that leads to the Beloved of all the worlds.

Pray thus to God, or the God you don't believe exists, for the illumination and guidance to recognize the Manifestation of God for this, your Day of emergence on this shore of consciousness, to come to the Primal Point that leads to Paradise.

This is the zenith of conscious-awareness, the coalescence of a physiologically-based state with one's Divine condition, that realizes our True nature, purpose, and the significance of living a dream within a Dream, a Simulator and Trainer meant to offer True Freedom, and the ability to Remember and Return to one's True Self once and for all times.

Holy Spirit

Ask and ye shall receive.
Ask the Holy Spirit, the Wave
On thy small wave, to heal,
And thou shalt be healed.
Ask from thy Spirit
To heal thy Spirit.

Ask from thy Soul
To heal thy pathway
To thy Soul.
Let God do the healing.
Let the Creator of all
Heal His creature.

He knows what to heal,
And what to let be,
For the Tree of Knowledge
Grows in His back yard.

His is the Soil
That nurtures the Life
Of every planet,
Every individual
Cell, molecule,
Atom.

Adam was not the first or last
Adam.
He has been and always will be,
As all the Names of God.
Listen carefully within.
What name has God picked
For you to embody?
The blood pumping
In and out of your heart,
With a soft sound,
Keeps whispering
Your name.

Breathe in, breathe out.
Ask,
"What is my name?"
When that name appears

In your Heart of hearts,
Guard its brilliance
In the secret cave
Of your inner Knowingness.
Its brightness will
Shine forth
In every deed,
Thought, and feeling
As you bend like bamboo—
Bowing before God's Breath
Of perfect
Change.

A Change in the Weather

The colors of the rainbow
Sift through the mist
Of illusion, allowing
God's Plan to emerge
Gradually, ray upon
Colored ray of hope
For a humanity
That wanders in the dark,
Unaware that soon

The full sun will break
Through, shattering
The sky's emptiness
With a new world
Of possibilities—the endless
Blessings of dawn songs,
Myriads of new birds
Calling to each other
With trills and high chirps
Announcing,
"The King is here.
The Earth is saved.
The people celebrate
The coming tide of Joy."

God's Will

The Will of God is found Written in His own Book(s), progressive and gradual Dispensations of His Mercy and Grace over all His creatures, extending an invitation to those whose Faith-full-ness is a sincere and truthful expression of His Divine Plan.

The travelers' conditional expression of Knowing-ness and Loving-ness will always be challenged and guided towards a higher sphere of Understanding and Love, as each traveler is inched closer to the Beloved of all the worlds. These conditional transformations, Spiritual in nature, open greater panoramic insights into the worlds of Revelation, worlds that are both a promise and the only Reality within and through one's Soul-based state of pure awareness. Thus, the traveler becomes acquainted with the transcendental nature of his or her own Reality.

The Movement of Love

The triangle that a tree makes
Is God at the Top Point,
And an eternal companion at each point
Below makes the Foundation.

The Sunlight of God
Permeating the First Point
Descends both sides of the triangle,
Then connects

The points of these two eternal servants
With His love and Wisdom.

In gratefulness they
Rise and Return to Him.
In this way our Creator

Loves Him-Self within the infinity
Of the Point,
Through the Sacred triangle
Of the Tree.

Preventing the needed tranquility and harmony
of all the members, living and non-living, who share

this planet, His creatures known on Earth _as human by agreement_, by choosing their own wills over His Will, are the cause of the pestering and tormenting, troubling, afflicting, and persecuting problems of the planetary system of Life and Intelligence.

When the _Written Will and Pleasure of the Creator_ is ignored and violated in many ways, resisted and debased, desecrated and dishonored, infringed upon and disobeyed, the likely outcome should not surprise anyone. We have broken the Structure that supports all Life and Intelligence, brought about by cross-contamination and pollution engulfing everything in its wake, and disrupted the flow of energetics that manifest well-being and harmony as components of the tranquility, transparency, and functionality of each individual. We have profoundly disturbed the collective in all its components: all its members' interactions and relationships. We have thereby masked the beauty of the face of Life and Intelligence, from within and from without, throughout the trans-dimensional and multi-directional aspects of this planet, as it relates to a community of planetary Life and Intelligence within this galaxy.

Travelers have behaved as if their actions carry no consequences—ever—while pursuing over the course of their imprisonment within the Simulator and

Trainer every ill-conceived desire and exaggeration that disregards every idea that leads to amicable cooperation. The necessary trust and consultation that fosters justice and peace within their species, and within the environment shared with every other species is destroyed, disturbing the very core that maintains all life on Earth, including the soil, air, and water that supply all its organisms, individually and collectively.

Yet, despite the creatures' rebelliousness, ignorance, and mismanaged passions creating every expression of imperfection and journeys of separation from the ideal goal, they will be guided to find their ways towards their ultimate objective—knowing their Higher Selves and Stations in the scheme of His Creation.

Oneness of Being speaks of that which exists within, the creation of God. An instant product of His Will and Pleasure, *Oneness of Manifestation* is that which will get expressed in worlds of time, the work-in-progress translating through the flux of energy/matter a perfect copy over time. Through this process the traveling entity explores and discovers his or her inner-Self, understanding thus the Love of the Creator Who Desires to be Known.

The tug-of-wills (the Creator's and creature's) becomes the essence of opposites: what is right and what is wrong; what is beautiful and what is not; an experience that is both an objective expression in the theater of existence within a Simulator and Trainer, and a subjective realization that allows for the varying expressions of myriad details, the melody and cacophony of endless possibilities that orchestrate Life and Intelligence; an experiment that ultimately leads back to a beginning that has no beginning— wakefulness in the Realm of Eternity, where everything was, and is, ever-present, always.

Light

In the beginning,
Before the Earth was formed,
God thought to Him-Self,
"I would like wonder
To appear everywhere.
I would like a Being,
Created in My Image,
To experience that wonder."
So here we are, in the year—,
And we have forgotten
The Beauty, the wonderment,

The original Purpose
Of our lives.

Let's live again
With God's Purpose
For each of our lives,
Leading us on
To the shining Kingdom
Of the Soul.

Let's allow our inner
Knowingness, filled with the life
The Creator placed
Within the heart
Of each of His Creatures,
To blossom forth
As the most Radiant Garden
Containing an infinite
And astounding variety
Of every kind and color of flower
Blowing and bending
In the breeze
Of His Loving-kindness.

Let's allow our-Selves
To shine forth—unhindered
By useless thoughts of power,
Prestige, or self-aggrandizement.

This is the time
To allow the inner trumpet calls
Of His Voice
To echo within the cavernous
Chambers of each one's
Eternal Beingness!

This is the time
To receive the strengthening rays
Of the golden Inner Sun
That illumines all
Who sincerely pray
For the Great Spirit's
Eternal up-lift-ment
And Mercy.
The Great Mystery
Needs no one, yet gives
To all—each according
To his or her capacity and station.

Let His Grace rain down,
A beneficent benediction
Of blessings,
To uplift the weary traveler
From eons of mortal lives,
So that he and she may
Rejoice to see and hear
With His Eyes and Ears,
And touch with the gentle
Firmness of the Master.

Though worlds may turn
Through misery and mayhem,
He—the Invincible One—
Stands at the Gate of the Heart
Ready to Pour Forth
Legions of Light-filled
Angels to break the bonds
Of self and desire
With one thought:
<u>Know thy-Self</u>
<u>And know Me.</u>

All systems of Intelligence and Life require the information that leads to the work being done. Travelers are informed through, first of all, He Who God makes Manifest for a period of development. The Revealed Word becomes the first of two entry points: A Dispensation that brings forth both omni-dimensional and multi-directional changes, influencing an epigenesis of growth, collectively. The second entry point is the Soul-based modulation upon each individual carrier-wave, acting upon those that are connected and integrated, consciously. This last imposition of Divine Information defines the traveler's identity, as a Being of Light in transit, Soul-possessing, seeker of the Truth, during his or her sojourn's fractional and temporal, existential experience. Without it, the traveler defines him- or her- self in whichever way any and all Earthly circumstances occur.

Since the object of the Journey is to _graduate_, that is, to become illumined and fully cognizant of one's True Self, to Remember thus and Return, away from the Simulator and Trainer, any egoic-programming simply delays it. It is important to understand that becoming a servant of the Creator, rather than of the egoic-self, is the highest goal of the Journey, and brings about a super-positioning of God's Will—_as it is done in Heaven, so it is done on Earth_.

This process is none other than the *Oneness of Being*, God's inner Perfections, given to the traveler through the engraved Soul within, followed by the *Oneness of Manifestation*, a oneness reflected *outwardly*, without the interference and corruption of the egoic-self. When enough enlightened beings exhibit a Oneness of Manifestation, the Earth becomes a *perfect mirror* reflecting the attributes and qualities of a Heavenly Domain.

The traveling entities simply must take *the First Step in the Right Direction* for God's Will and Mercy to show forth the early stages of a *new creation*. Illumined by God, doing His Will and Pleasure, they are of the Chosen!

A *new story* begins, and a new cycle of thousands of years is set in motion: *The Dawn of the Age of Maturity* of humanity. This is, in truth, an unavoidable stage in the process of Remembering and Returning to one's True Self.

Travelers have been through this process, time and again; they just haven't remembered it. Some have begun the *True Awakening* by having responded to the *Clarion Call* of the Beloved of all the worlds.

Arise then, and fulfill your Divine Destiny, and be counted among the Blessed!

Nectar

Inside the heart
Of each true human being
Is a longing for the Love
Of the Infinite One.
When all the flotsam
And jetsam of life's
Infinite tests and trials
Is cleared away,
The blue sky
Of all possibilities
Shines forth
From that Center
Of human awareness.
Then the longing
(For His Love—the Infinite
Mystery of total
Abundance) impels each
Creature to bow, willow-like,
To the One Singleness—
God's Glory—
Dissolving in the Ocean
Of many-splendored

Love
As butterflies
Disappear
In the many-colored,
Lifted flower petals
Of His Grace.

Four Stories

There are four, _concurrently running films_, programs within the Simulator and Trainer. These four patterns can be thought of as _stories_, scripts representing and expressing the inner, developmental conditions of the inhabitants of a _Planetary System of Life and Intelligence_, anywhere, and at any time.

The act of creation, from the Creator's point of view, is one of making Himself Known to the creature, and as such, these four stories represent the gradual conscious awareness of the creature, a traveling entity, as a process of the _realization of His Presence_, through His Love within.

The _first of these four stories_ represents the lowest form of behavior, a conduct or performance below that of the animal, activities predominantly instinctive, and lacking all spiritual connection to the fifth-dimensional state, individually and collectively. An individual acting from the first story exhibits a fourth-dimensional state (mind, energies, and time) subservient to an egoic-condition that knows no boundaries. It is a life-style totally and completely self-serving, destructive to self and others, filled with violence, corruption, deception, mindlessness, and heartlessness. The first story always leads entities into conflict. It disrupts the basis of unity and tranquility of the family, the community, the city, the state, the nation, and the world. Individuals enmeshed in the first story cannot consult to achieve the necessary, common goal of an ever-advancing Divine Civilization.

The first story is the realm of the *dead of Soul and Spirit*. Its inhabitants are purposeless, living a meaningless life, a *hell on Earth*, without hope or the understanding that there is a better life in an Eternal Realm that could begin right now simply with a *first act* of Righteousness—His Love is always there, though they know it not.

These inhabitants are in need of *the Word of God*— to be resurrected and be reconnected with the Spirit of Life and Intelligence of the Universe. Through the Word of God, the unbeliever will rise above the fray of uselessness and corruption, will be released from acting as the evil-doers, the oppressors, and the wicked, in order to join, one-by-one, *the second story's* higher layer of activity, as connected with the Spirit of the imperceptible field of activities supporting the life of the mineral, plant, animal, and human Kingdoms on Earth.

These individuals of the second story, though connected with the Spirit of Life and Intelligence, are in further need of _quickening_, or integration with their Soul-based states of awareness. From being dead (the first story), they have now become sleepy (the second story). By being increasingly modulated by their Soul-based point-of-view, they can move up spiritually (ascend in Knowingness and Lovingness) within the second story towards the level of the third story.

As entities of the second story ascend closer towards the tenth-dimensional state of the True Self, they experience the gradual removal of the veils of ignorance and vain imagining interposed between _an actuality of illusions_, and _a Reality that never ceases to be_.

The temporal pales in contrast, then, with the Eternal; impermanence fades before the light of a permanence that offers a continuing state of peace and stability, in the Light of an inner and outer justice that is ever-present.

The inhabitants of this _second story_, and world, have an incomplete understanding of the purpose of the Simulator and Trainer, the world of time they are a part of, and live within. They come and go in different worlds of time, time and again, and have never asked themselves the reason for, and nature of their journeys. These inhabitants have yet to be Chosen to be a part of the *third story* or script. Their opinions are a mix of half-truths and facts, in their attempts to describe the world around them. They exist in partial darkness, towards the entrance of the cave. Not until the sun shines through its opening will those of the second story be able to see clearly enough to distinguish right from wrong. Even with a mental knowledge of moral and ethical principles, second story inhabitants, without the full Presence of the Divine within, will be unable to sustain right action.

In the second story, there is a tug-of-war between one's own will and the Will of God, between righteous actions and malice, or the evil done in the name of whatever justifies it.

Residents of the second story or scripts played as roles, if Chosen, rise above the fray of those afflicted by the contrast of ideas and actions into the light of a continuum of right ideas, right actions, and right feelings.

These latter travelers have entered the *world or Plane of Limitations*, as restrictions that emerge out of their existing spiritual capacities, a limited state of Knowingness and Lovingness that still veils the glory and splendor of true emancipation, the enlightenment that follows their Spiritual growth within this world of understanding and actions, a heart-felt presence of the Creator, as a Guide that continuously offers the Light and Comfort a _New Manifestation_ of His Splendor brings. It is then, when the traveler and seeker of the Truth has come face-to-face with His Creator, through His Manifestation, that he or she begins a process that will take him or her to the _summit of conscious-awareness_.

In this _third story_, the traveler and seeker of the Truth finds the struggle inherent in the Law of God within him or her, the need to obey in order to reach the heights of unity and harmony within a social common-wealth of interactions: goods and services produced and exchanged, and personal relationships in the light of His Justice.

Gradually, each traveling entity grows in Spirituality and Understanding, removing his or her earlier inherent limitations derived from wrong ideas and erroneous feelings, and comes to be a part of _the fourth story_: Oneness of Being and Manifestation: _The Plane of Oneness_, as a blessing of God.

Unencumbered by ignorance, vain imaginings, and unmanaged passions, the entity returns to his or her True Self, as an eternal servant of God, living within the precincts of His Love.

Lifted

Beyond the farthest mountain
Of doubt and despair
Lies the Sea of Faith
That cannot be stirred
By any thought or action
And instead is Animated
By the longing for God's Love
In every particle
Of one's Being.

Plunged in the waters
Of this Divine Dispensation,
The traveler to worlds
Upon worlds
Of illusion and false desires
Is released into the freedom
Of this Love—
And like a sailing ship
With sails filled with the winds
Of divine destiny—
Slips across the waves
Knowingly

To reach the shores
Of Certitude.

Without a doubt
This Love
Solves all the problems
So that the Light of Being
Stands tall as a Beacon
For those in the night of error,
Shining with the Faith
In the Unknowable One
To the extent that the whole
Ocean of Life
Bends and bows
To God's Beauty,
Quickened to life
And lit by Divine Guidance
In a mass entrance
Through the Gates
Of Paradise.

Praise Be
To the Creator's Mercy
And Love,

Inspiring the entire creation
To be lifted
Back
Into its original,
Perfect
Form—
Glory to the All-Glorious.

End of the Journey

Wandering through worlds of time,
The traveler pauses
Only for an instant:
Lightning bolt of knowledge
Passes through the mortal
Frame.
In an instant—Awakening!
Eons of struggle disappear
Before the Immortal Beauty
Of the Mysterious Presence.
Ego dissolves into nothingness.
Self rises like the Sun—
His Image

Is reflected everywhere,
Like water in the hollowed-out
Cup of a lake,
Spreading the sunrise sky,
Hugging the Earth.

For some reason, inexplicably,
Joy creeps in,
A whispered Promise,
Mom speaking softly to babe
She cuddles close.

Love is as natural
As the Earth turning—
And as imperceptible.

"Come close, come close,
Dear one,"
The Creator whispers
In the heart of each creature.
All is well.

The *fourth story* is a true expression of His Will on an Earthly plane. Traveling entities, now true servants of the Lord of all the worlds, enhance and assist in the advancement of a Divine Civilization. Their conduct and actions help others, over time, realize their True Selves. They carry the power to bring true change to all the areas forgotten by the egoic actions of the dead and sleepy. The super-positioning of beauty and harmony begins to appear, as these travelers participate in every community and city. Slowly at first, encumbered by the ill-will present in the empty hearts of those living in the first and second stories who resist the potential change offered while opposing the Beauty of the Beloved, the Enlightened ones of the _fourth story_ raise the consciousness of society.

For those that have eyes to see and ears to listen, the sight of such drama and hardship, as particularly propels those immersed within the first and the second stories, portends the opening of a door that brings the Promise of a New Day—the end of Winter and the beginning of Spring.

Hidden/Revealed

The longing in the heart
For the Beloved
Never stops.
Sometime it is hidden

By the noise
Of worldly distractions, vain delusions.
Other times
His Voice calls—we answer,
Like chicks to mother hen
Soul-running
To the Soul-Maker.

Turn within
And listen....
There, in the time-less, place-less point,
The Dot of Eternity,
Blooms
His ever-flowering, All-Glorious
Presence—stamped
On our very Be-ing-ness
As lightning etches
Its searing path
On the stormy sky.

Many travelers, within the Simulator and Trainer, in response to their longing for the Best Beloved, find themselves in a loop that knows no end. Longing becomes their goal, and separation, the way and method.

This world is filled with gurus, yogis, fakirs, swamis, saints, and the like, whose search for the Creator has rendered a myriad paths and experiences that will eventually lead to the realization that unless an entity is Chosen, the way is eternally barred.

The _Unknowable Essence_ reveals Himself to whomever He chooses, and not the other way around.

Endless lives in search of the Beloved of all the worlds may pass. The seeker will experience what he deems to be Divine as the source of his or her quest. Yet, despite all that effort, all that time and ways, the _Ultimate Reflection of His Will_ shall remain Hidden.

The Creator reveals Himself in Whomever He Chooses. Those that are His Chosen Ones are the Manifestations of His Divine Plan. These Divine Entities appear once in a great while, and when They do, His creation is transformed anew, and _all of His creatures_ are given the opportunity to advance. This advancement is by degrees, within whichever of the four stories they each inhabit. Some, those whose existence revolves around the first story, may be Chosen to be a part of one of the other three. The same applies to the members of the other three stories; those that are chosen will abide within a story that reflects their new condition of nearness to the Beloved.

This gradual process of True Remembrance and Return to one's True-Self becomes thus a reflection of the Creator's Will and Pleasure _on whomever He has chosen to illumine_.

True Awakening and Enlightenment, Remembering and Returning, is all up to the Creator, Who does what He Wills and Pleases, on whomsoever He chooses.

This has been His way from the beginning that has no beginning, and will continue to be His way till the end that has no end. Only God knows what lies within each heart and within each mind. He alone is able to discern the state of being of each of His creatures and differentiate among their needs and desires.

Dispensations

In preparation to be of the Chosen, and as a part of the Journey of separation, Remembrance, and Return to one's True-Self, a traveling entity must be guided to *the only way* and means to that end.

Through the Creator's successive Revelations of His Will and Pleasure, a Divine Plan becomes known to His creatures, those earmarked for Illumination. This Divine process aids the lost to regain the confidence, clarity, and understanding required to have access to his or her salvation. That is, the pathway makes ready each entity to be Chosen, and be removed from the Simulator and Trainer's four stories, at some moment in time and place known only to Himself.

To regain one's intended station, known only to God, becomes the ultimate reason and highest aspiration of the seeker of the Truth—through obedience to His Will and Pleasure, only.

And so, the Journey began, a test of faithfulness and sincerity for every entity, every Being of Light,

Soul-possessing, Spirit of Life and Intelligence, a potential in transit and transcendence, and a seeker of the Truth that is Self-awareness, and through that process, a means to that end, grow in Knowingness and Lovingness, as a servant of his or her Creator.

Of the unknown numbers of Dispensations of Divine Energy and Information throughout His Creation, locally, here on Earth, the last four of the last Adamic Cycle are worthy of mention. These are the Revelations of Moses, the Law giver; Buddha the Enlightened One; Jesus, son of Mary; and Muhammed, the Apostle of God; for they each emphasize a specific aspect of the _Straight Path_ leading to the Glory of God.

Hence, within the Simulator and Trainer, these four Dispensations of Divine Information, whose main themes are Obedience to the Law, Righteousness and Compassion, Love and Forgiveness, Submission and Surrender, respectively, when viewed together, contain the four prerequisites for advancement towards enlightenment—the understanding of Love.

Further, it is the _sum-total of all Four Ways_ to nearness to the All-Mighty One that gives each Light Being the best opportunity to advance spiritually, pointing to the significance of the Unity and Oneness of all His Manifestations.

As a consequence of this realization, the traveling entity clearly understands that any distinction among, or refusal to accept any One of, the Manifestations of One God, or any attempt to deny that They are One-and-the-Same, nullifies the intended result or benefit to be found through any one of Their Dispensations. The seeker either acknowledges this Oneness and Unity of God and His Manifestations, or he or she is lost within the mirage of vain imaginings as a consequence of this error of perspective and judgment.

This incorrect viewpoint alone, time and again, has been the source of separation and fragmentation of the minds and hearts of all the inhabitants everywhere, and at all times. The Root Source of Unity and Oneness, that serves as a Framework for the acquisition of the right tools that bring about the unification of Self, family, community, city, state, nation, and a world commonwealth, is absent.

As a result, we see a conflagration of symptoms that clearly tells its own script, an actuality that is palpably written and acted upon across the plains of human interaction and relationships, emerging as the four stories play the gamut of possible outcomes, time and again.

This senseless and aimless scenario of endless games played, that always leads to self-destruction, is based upon the incorrect assumption that entities are _co-creators_ with the _Creator_, and results in a seamless actuality of gross, unmanaged passions, an ocean of collective consciousness drowning in its own filth and despair.

Despite the ever-present solution available through the last four Dispensations of Divine Energy and Information, the travelers have opted to follow their own whims and desires, again.

The way of the Law and Obedience, the way of Righteousness and Compassion, the way of Love and Forgiveness, and the way of Submission and Surrendering are all but One Dictum from a Creator that Loves His creatures. They represent the way to the Glory of God—through their effect on the human character and conduct, and its influence on the advancement of civilization and overall human destiny, as sealed by His Will and Pleasure.

It's amusing that these ways are simply _common-sense_, encouraging ways of thinking, feeling, and acting that the human inhabitants of Earth continue to ignore at their peril.

Instead, humanity chooses to listen to the falsehoods and denials whispered in every heart, from the pulpits of those desiring power. The multitudes of simple-hearted and simple-minded individuals, grouped in innumerable communities, continue to be misled, while waiting for their salvation.

In the beginning

When the world was young,
Humans walked upon the Earth
Remembering their Creator.
Over time, as the lure of the senses
Gained ascendancy,
They forgot to Whom
They owed allegiance.

Now, in these dark
And perilous times,
The opportunity has come
For each entity to Return
To his or her Origin—
As a brilliant Beacon,
An eternal Being of Light
Bowing within each heart
To the Almighty One

Who created each of us
From His Unfathomable
Love.

Are you ready for
The Journey?
Have you packed your bags
Of virtues, jettisoned
That which no longer
Serves
The All-Knowing One?

The One singleness Who
Created the multitudes
Of creatures
Is always near-at-hand,
Extending infinite rays
Of unbounded Joy
For our drooping Souls
To climb upon
And hitch a ride
Back to the Source
Of our True-Selves.

Waste no time.

For the inhabitants of the first and second stories, their mind-world constructs as traveling entities, what each one of them understands of life, is the outcome or after-effect of myriad programs originating mostly from the world around them, as well as from each one's egoic-self, to the degree of their ignorance, and as the effect of their mismanaged energetics and desires.

These are basic third- and fourth- dimensional inputs that converge as information that builds the memories acted upon by the individual traveler. There is little or no input or flow of information from the fifth-dimensional state, the Spirit of Life and Intelligence of the Universe, on the inhabitants of that world. The result is that the system of Life and Intelligence most people experience, conditioned as it is only as the effect of those environmental, temporal restrictions, and egoical-self impositions, out of the darkness of their ignorance, limits the range and scope of these entities' understanding and feelings. They are deprived of the condition and capacity—mentally, emotionally, and spiritually—necessary to live and advance in peaceful co-existence with others.

Instead, against God's Plan for all His creatures, these entities act from a lack of virtues. Their biological feed-back becomes one of violence and competition, anger and resentment, oppression and wickedness, deceit and falsehoods, half-truths and misunderstanding. The programming that emerges within, as their mind-world constructs and feelings, represents the only world they experience.

As prisoners of this quagmire or quicksand of predicaments and entanglements, they are obviously doomed from the start. Any entity born in this environment, statistically speaking, cannot escape its inherent drama. He or she is destined for failure— unless and until _the Word of God_, unadulterated and pure, unsullied by the misinterpretation of outsiders, untainted and unmodified by egoic-selves, reaches the heart of each inhabitant and re-programs that Being: the feelings, understandings and mind-world constructs. The Word of the Messengers reawakens every Spirit through the Elixir of Life, recreating thus the fundamental clarity and functionality of each entity back to its original state.

The value of _Prayers_, as originally Revealed, have that effect upon any of the inhabitants of the four stories. In each case, and to a prescribed measure, as a means to an end, the appropriate changes (re-programming at the Root-level) occur.

Adding to this initial correction and attunement (necessary adjustments to the instrumentation of each Being), and by realigning the basic components of body, mind, Spirit, and Soul, the integration that brings the Whole to the part, the Revealed Text or Books of the latest Manifestation of God, provide the needed Divine Information that re-programs the traveling entity's way, as an observer and as a participant. He or she, who was lost within the egoic-self's mind-world construct and veiled heart, finds the guiding Light and compass redirecting and bringing purpose and meaning to his or her life.

In short, the flow of Divine Information and Energetics, from the latest Dispensation of God, recreates those that are chosen for salvation. The tug-of-war between the delusional will of the traveler, and God's Will, stands in the way of any progress.

Similarities

The entities coming and going, to and from temporal worlds, have fallen into a delusion and misconception, an aberration or false impression, a misunderstanding and mirage conceived of as _reality_, based on the dissimilarities and superficial variations and contrast as the basis for judgment. They then respond with actions and words that describe the experience, building mind-world constructs in ways that antagonize those participating in any and all situations, rather than using the tools that create a bridge of _natural unity_ across the surface of diversity.

The predominance of entities utilizing ways of thinking and feelings that emphasize the apparent differences among His creatures reduces each and all the participants into beings that face, from day to day, an ever-growing, insurmountable dilemma and crisis: one that has to deal with all of our differences, real and imagined, born of culture or of ritual, made into mythology and tradition, predicaments of prejudice, of ignorance, and emotional imbalance.

Instead of exploring, discovering, and using the similarities present in all of us, a familiarity that prevents the assumptions that have brought so much suffering, these travelers have fallen prey to a short-sighted point of view that has kept alive a system of understanding that is abusive and violent for hundreds of thousands of years.

Seeing our similarities helps us to welcome the stranger, extend a hand to the down-trodden, the young and old everywhere, and eradicate conflicts and wars among the members of a family or a community, between neighbors or even among nations, so that we may share harmonious and productive lives on one planet we call our home.

What are the parameters of _a familiarity_ with each other that are complete enough and sufficiently clear and adequately robust to enable us to crush the artificial barriers we have built to separate each Being's mind and heart from another's?

Speak-up, oh people of understanding!

We share so many aspects of our-Selves, defining who we are and applicable to all the places (planets) offering temporary shelters to all of us traveling within worlds of time....

None of us are strangers, no matter our temporary planetary homes, or the differences in culture, language, or even units of travel. Instead, viewed as entities, we are all eternal companions, creatures of one Creator, as our True Selves. We are immortal, illumined Beings, Soul-possessing Spirits of Life and Intelligence, seeing with the Eyes, hearing with the Ears, and carrying within the Voice of the same Creator.

We are seekers of the Truth, potentials transiting vast, multi-dimensional universes, ever-growing in Knowingness and Lovingness as the servants of God.

Being familiar with our weighty and significant similarities, we can see our surface, apparent differences for what they are—simply the spices of life that give each Light Being a slightly different mission, in the same honorable service promoting the advancement of a divine civilization according to the Will and Pleasure of the Great Spirit.

Immersed

As the river flows
Through the winding way,
Our destinies meander us
Past virtues and vices

To the One Meadow
Where the Nightingale sings
A Song of Oneness.

Who cannot help but be
Delighted
As the Song of Unity
Pours forth,
Describing every bird
And flower
In the "language of
Birds"—liquid, trilling melodies
That weave together
The listening hearts
Of True Seekers.

Each Being
Climbing the ladder
Towards God's Grace
Is filled with Endless
Joy, for there is no purpose
Greater than plunging,
Head-long,
Into the Sky

Reflected in the Ocean
Of Wonder,
Immersing one's Self
In the rippling waves
Of His Love
And Wisdom, encircled
By the shores
Of His Grace.

From this familiar array of fundamental similarities identifying every Soul-possessing creature, the traveling entity is better equipped to honor our dissimilar features, such as languages, traditions and rituals, beliefs and roles, and the like.

As each creature _descends_ intra-dimensionally to its point of entry within the Simulator and Trainer, a dream within a Dream, until its final return to its True-Self, a simultaneous journey of exploration and discovery with untold others everywhere, and at all times, is taking place. Each traveler increasingly experiences the worlds of Revelation from within, and the worlds that Manifest the initial and fundamental Oneness from without. Accepting and confirming the existence of the many worlds of God, the traveler

grows in Knowingness and Lovingness, in a state of
ever-growing nearness, approaching the Beloved.

Love and Grace

As the sun rises every day,
As the mountain stands steady
Through eons,
As the rivers keep flowing
To the sea,
Thy Love
Holds us steady, gently,
In Its Almighty grasp,
With endless patience,
Until we rise from our beds
Of heedlessness,
Remembering
Our True Natures
And Birth-place:
Thy Grace rocking us
Back into our Selves,
Attracted as hummingbirds
To the sweetest nectar
Of the brilliant, red-pink

Flowers standing tall
Against the blue, summer
Sky.

Through the exploration and discoveries made from within, _the Oneness of Being_, of the individual and of humankind, is propelled into a process, within the Simulator and Trainer, that catapults this _Planet's System of Life and Intelligence_ towards a conscious awareness, linearly and non-linearly (within and outside the flow of time), merging and integrating, first, within the community of _Planetary Systems of Life and Intelligence_, then leading to the eventual and final integration of all consciously aware entities within a _Galactic System of Life and Intelligence_. Such a process, to last five hundred thousand years, is the first of many super-cycles integrating our _Universal System of Life and_ _Intelligence_.

The Divine Plan of the Creator begins with the inner merging and integration of all entities within a _Planetary System of Life and Intelligence._ This synthesis is no small task indeed, as to obtain the state of cognition of the _Oneness of Being_ within entails a process that integrates one's Soul-based state with the Spirit of Life and Intelligence of the Universe, as well as with one's mind and body. The result is the bringing forth of one's True Self to the interactive arena of the material world, so that each entity's True Self is *expressed* with every other Being's True Self in a *Oneness of Manifestation.*

The outward expression of Oneness derived from the Soul-based viewpoint is necessary as the foundation for the spiritual and material state of world unity.

The ensuing world-commonwealth allows for the unifying of the contrasting and diverse differences of its traveling entities to form an *eternal companionship* connecting each Being to an ever-advancing, and never-ending. trans-dimensional Civilization, a Reality that exists, and has always existed, tenth-dimensionally speaking as the Creator's Intent.

This global Spiritual and Soul-based transformation, creation-wide, was, and is, the Purpose of God's Revelations, from a beginning that knows no beginning, until an end that knows no end.

With each Dispensation of Divine Information, throughout the one thousand Adamic Cycles experienced on this Planetary System of Life and Intelligence, each divine *pit-stop*, one of many, has served as a Spiritual training and educational facility, leading all entities towards a cosmological integration the like of which, linearly-speaking (time wise), we have never experienced.

The journey towards this _Objective_ has proved extremely difficult and trying.

However, the time to leave behind our adolescent collective behavior is over, and a new stage and phase in our collective understanding started around the middle of the nineteenth century, when human capacity was augmented one-hundred-fold.

Our ability to understand both our material environment, and our Spiritual condition, knows no declared limits within the Intelligent Design. The Divine Plan proceeds as an expression of His Will and Pleasure.

Birth

Along with the ocean waves
Pounding against the shore,
Our thoughts repeat
In endless cycles
Until we are freed
From the incessant repetition
Of patterns, our thoughts falling
In myriad drops of salty water
Disappearing into the sandy,
Wavy shoreline

As our Spirits rise like mist
Towards the compassionate Sun.

There, in the sky of Eternity,
Like eagles circling
Craggy nest
Atop the snow-tipped mountain,
We collide as we land
Together—One
In our ever-expanding
Home.
God is calling us
To Return,
Leave everything behind,
Let no obstacle
Block our soaring
Into the Bright Realms,
Invisible.

We wing our ways
Towards Heaven
Until we land
At His Feet, bowing
Within, grateful

For a chance to rest
Without thought,
Simply basking
In the Radiant Sun-Light
Of His Presence.

Sky-Light

Deep in the well of the Soul,
Beyond thinking,
Beyond feeling,
Beyond Understanding,
Is the Knowingness
That we are all One.

Here, in the deep recesses
Of Light, past worlds upon
Worlds of lives lived, cave-like,
In semi-darkness, we emerge
Onto the open plain
Of His expanding Grace.
The Lord's Will holds forth
On every heart.
Every Light-Being reflects back

Divine Love
So that worlds upon worlds
Of Revelation
Rise up like mountains
Bursting through roof-less
Skies.

Travelers, however, must be consciously aware about the actuality being perceived and participated in. There is a descriptive layering, embedded and enfolded. All of its components must be properly identified and included when we formulate a plan of action or decision. When inadvertently omitting or committing acts that ignore or violate its inner and outer properties, as well as their concurrent influences on other aspects of the actuality being experienced, we deliver a catastrophic result. We are connected to everything and everyone; the flow of energetics and information must remain unchanged and unrestricted, just as it originated from its Source.

Everything that is good originates from God.

Thus, the Spiritual and causative components, as imperceptible fields of activity, cannot be disregarded in their entirety, or partially, when formulating mental constructs that will, over time, become expressed in the material world.

Fifth-dimensional (spiritually-based) influxes, unless included in their fullness, on a fourth-dimensional state (of mind, energy, and time), in turn, affecting third-dimensional constructs, will undermine and create unstable structures, be they mental or physical expressions of thought-designs meant to advance civilization.

Entities that are disconnected from, or partially connected to, the Spirit of Life and Intelligence of a locality, group, region, or a planet, as members of the first and second stories, are incapable of clearly and coherently functioning or producing anything of worth for the social structure and time-line they are a part of.

It is important to understand the implications of any and all interactions and relationships that emerge from those travelers whose lack of well-being renders them unable to think and feel in a manner that will sustain activities that contribute to the Whole. The world, as an arena and theater of activities, amply testifies to the compounded effects derived from those entities who find themselves in such a desperate spiritual situation. They are simply beings whose incomplete structuring and integration of the levels of the body, mind, Spirit, and Soul disallows their ability to see and hear the complete layering of an actuality all around them. Their mind-world constructs become erroneously programmed and charged with the absence of appropriate emotional responses to everyday activities.

There are four worlds to consider: the material, the mental, the Spiritual, and the Soul-based state of awareness. Together, these four present each traveler sets of independent layers, embedded and construed as a single frame of reference in order for us to have a clear understanding of the world of time shared, as we constantly interact with others whose understandings must be in agreement as expressions of a commonwealth that exists within the nature of who we all are.

When an entity is an expression of his or her state of Oneness of Being, God's creation allows that condition to express itself as a Oneness that manifests, without the distortions of an egoically-modulated carrier wave, that is, without the programming that distorts or damages the flow transmitting his or her inner attributes. Clarity and coherence bring to bear, then, an adequate and complete picture and frame of reference to work with—as an individual, and as a member of a family, community, city-state, nation, and the world. The information from the most comprehensive and perfect Source is being allowed to merge and integrate with the other three aspects of the actuality experienced.

There is an empirical history or story that describes mankind's time on Earth. It deals with evolution and survival. It results from our scientific inquiry that presents snaps of time, clips derived from cognitive patterns as they are lived within an environment. This story does not address any introjection or influence emanating from outside the Simulator and Trainer— the delivery of the Creator's Revelations and its inherent effect on those societies, and the reason that the low degree of spiritual evolution, its cyclic scheme, repeats itself.

It is thus a relative view, limited by the empirical evidence discovered, leaving out the implications and messages found through the *spiritual history or story* of mankind's spiritual growth, taking place in direct relation to the advent of God's Manifestations. It is this *poorly and incompletely understood spiritual story* that is the one responsible for the *True Advancement* of civilization.

Viewed from a Spiritual perspective, universal and all inclusive, we can observe four, generalized characteristics that, when assembled, integrated over time, and superposed as continuing events that give rise to the way things are and have always been, make sense of a world of time.

The fog of time-limited understanding that emerges from the incomplete empirical evidence, and a divided and often prejudicial attitude prevalent throughout the ages, have given rise to a disconnect from a Reality and True Purpose that the existential process and programmed phenomena of our mortal lives were meant to contain.

Furthermore, the results from an impaired and skewed Spiritual development has brought about myriad world-constructs, a disarray representing, time and again, a variety of opinions and the greatest obstacle to be removed and give way to the _Light of True Reason_.

Humanity has taken small steps forward towards its maturity, in the light of its Spiritual Development meant to represent the understanding and follow-up behavior that brings true freedom, as a means for its members to Remember and Return to their True Selves.

Here – Not Here

Below the deepest ocean
Is the wave of Power
Which is God's
That Wave upholds the structure

Of universes.
It flows
From eternity to eternity,
Nurturing every sub-atomic
Particle with the emblem
Of Divine Love.

Behold! Without this Wave,
Nothing would exist.
The universe
Stands on a point of Nothingness
That contains everything.
In this balance
The One God smiles,
Aware that all life—
His Gift—could disappear
In the blink of the Immortal
Eye.
Still, His infinite Compassion
Creates ripples of Love
Floating forever on the Sea
Of His Mercy.
Glory to the All-Glorious.

A Short Trip

At long last
The Creator of All
Invited me to His Mansion.
It was crowded
In the main Hall.
Everyone was there:
Two-headed beasts
As well as Angels.
It turns out
That everyone had always
Been there—the same Heart—
We just hadn't been able

To see each other!

What a joke,
Thinking we existed
In separate universes
When, in Reality,
We were jostling elbows.

In the Mansion
Everyone ate together

At a long, white, damask-covered
Table intricately embroidered
With heart-shaped leaves and blooming
Flowers along the border.
Our golden plates were filled
With ambrosial delicacies
Straight from Heaven's kitchens.

Everyone ate for enjoyment;
No one was hungry.
Then, time to head back.
"Listen," God whispered in my ear
As I strapped on my wings.
"The people have forgotten Me,
And even the Celestial Table.
They fight over every mortal crumb.
Will you remind them?"

"I'll do my best."
Bowing from my heart,
I tumbled back, landed
On the couch.

So, I ask,

Would you like to eat
At the Table
Of Love's Perfection?

The disarray representing, time and again, a variety of opinions and the greatest obstacle to be removed and give way to the *Light of True Reason* is the *Greatest Falsehood* ever lived—the Satan of all the Ages.

This, the greatest of all lies, through a myriad faces and modalities since the beginning that has no beginning, within the Simulator and Trainer, is none other than a disbelief and a denial of the Creator of All. And, beyond this simple disbelief and denial, there is the further misconception that His Will and Pleasure, on whomsoever he chooses, is but pure imagination.

No matter what we do, time and again, travelers have failed to realize that a civilization built on the violations of the Reality expounded by the latest Manifestation Himself will not succeed, and will implode due to its weak and faulty structure. The resulting societal disintegration affects the whole body-politic and its functions, throughout the entire Planetary System of Life and Intelligence that houses its diseased members.

This *Greatest Lie* raises and elevates many "saviors" to the role of false prophets, who promise the way to happiness. Instead they deliver, over time, the re-birth of an ancient loop and its nascent by-products, attachments that separate entities from each other, distorting the principle of Oneness of Being and Manifestation, as designed and implemented by the Creator's latest Manifestation. Instead of experiencing the resurrection of the Faith of God, and the subsequent Spiritual transformation, these leaders, modulated by their egoic-selves, advocate faith in anything that serves an illusory agenda, filled with what a present-day, social condition appears to demand.

Thus, we witness many *pseudo-scientific methods* and other *quasi-approaches*, half-truths, that, when combined with past rituals and traditions, long forgotten and now revived through their present re-interpretation and remodeling, use modern language to satisfy the appetite for instant gratification and material-based happiness so prevalent in the West.

Despite the fact that we are all surrounded by a slowly disintegrating and collapsing eco-system, losing everything dear to us, including our own health as well as the well-being of all living organisms sharing this Earthly habitat, we continue to ignore the Lie that is the cause of our fall from Grace.

This Lie inhabits the first two stories in a greater or lesser fashion, and is expressed through individual life-styles. The disbelief in, or quasi-acceptance of, the Creator's Living Proof of His Will and Pleasure— His latest Manifestation—is expressed through the inhabitants of the first and second stories choosing to act from their own egoically-based wills over the Will of the Creator.

Unfortunately, the volume of travelers inhabiting these less developed, spiritual conditions adversely affects the inhabitants of the third story, who have begun their spiritual transformation, as well as those integrated Light Beings inhabiting the fourth story while serving the Divine Plan.

For this reason, the True advancement of the social order towards its Spiritual maturity has been unnecessarily delayed and disrupted.

Living the *Greatest Lie* is but an expression of one's denial of, and dispute against, God's Will (as found in all the Sacred Writings). The traveler gives his or her own egoic-self's will precedence, running against what the Creator Himself has Revealed through His Latest Manifestation.

Let Thy Will, not mine, be done!

Awakening

Within the *Cosmic Egg* of time and space, the Simulator and Trainer, the True Seeker waits for Self-realization and beyond that, nearness to the Beloved of all the worlds.

The phenomenon of *separation* is accented with a plethora of contrast: light and shadow, good and evil, far and near, knowing and not knowing, coming and going, etc. What the seeker needs is to Remember and begin his or her journey of Return to the Higher Self.

This process of resurrection and gaining of eternal life can be seen and understood as God's Will and Pleasure on those that are chosen to become charged with the *Divine Power of illumination* that opens the previously hidden Realm outside the Simulator and Trainer—cracking the Cosmic Egg to let the Light in.

There is a pattern worth mentioning in the Spiritual history of any planetary system of Life and Intelligence. When this Spiritual history is observed as a River of Knowledge and Life, or Divine Information, running linearly in time, through many Dispensations or Revelations of the Word of the Creator, we can see how successive communities gather together those that respond and continue to respond to each newly-named Manifestation.

As the generations of travelers arrive, the Shepherd gathers His sheep, and each new community, in turn, identifies itself with its Founder. We cannot fail to acknowledge a fundamental characteristic separating each "community of the called," despite the initial Intention of unifying the whole of humankind.

Each community, having identified itself with an ebb of the River of Life's flow, creating thus its own shore of consciousness with an aspect of the fractional and temporal, existential experience, reflects an attachment to a way of life that is in itself contrary to the inner process as Designed.

The Grammarian and the Mystic Knower of each and every one of these communities come to rest at the conscious shores produced by the ebb of flowing Life-Waters. Whereas the Grammarian, steeped in a Book knowledge, stops and wonders if, in his journey of exploration and discovery, he should plunge into the Waters and cross to the other side, the Mystic Knower readily dives and swims across the Living

Waters onto the opposite shore. The Knower urges his or her companion,

"Jump in. Swim. Come on over to the other side!" The Mystic Knower understands that courage is needed to continue one's Self's journey of exploration and discovery.

Traveling entities are meant to acknowledge the Faith of the Creator as the ultimate Guide, and crossing the Waters that carry His Faith is what needs to be done, rather than taking a life-time pit-stop within one or another of these communities. Getting attached to time-specific rituals and traditions brings about a loop that knows no end, causing the seeker to identify with the fractional and temporal aspects of his or her journey, rather than focusing on its Eternal aspect. The ever-present embrace of a Whole allows for a larger transformation than any temporal and insignificant moment can provide.

To live in the eternal moment requires the traveler to be awakened to the Realization of the Self. The Higher Self lives elsewhere and cannot afford to get trapped in the names and appearances of every-day living. Glancing at the pattern of the many communities laid across a linear track of time shows the creation of sequentially-arranged, spiritual prisons containing living cargo conditioned by the interpretations of leaders *who falsely promise true freedom* from the maladies afflicting the rest of the world.

In fact, the only True Freedom lies and is found when crossing the Waters of Life. By plunging one's Higher Self into the Dispensation or Revelation brought by a Messenger of God, we can partake of the Divine Content and be transformed spiritually from the eternal experience that brings about Enlightenment, Remembering and Returning *through non-attachment*. By remaining an independent seeker of the Truth, and by identifying one's Self with the Oneness Principle of the Faith of God, as delivered by every Messenger, we become prepared for a future of further Deliveries, without the conditioned resistance and denial that results when attached to names and appearances.

By embracing the freedom to explore and discover, in order to achieve the Eternal, the traveling entity may partake of all the Dispensations of Divine Information, now, and in the future. Using this method, and depending only on the Creator, the Seeker of Truth acknowledges that these Dispensations require a Manifestation of God, His Messenger; yet the true Water of Life, the Knowingness, is found in the Message. In being able to distinguish the true meaning of that Freedom, a freedom that allows each Being to continue to partake of additional Divine portions of God's Plan, without the restraint and conditions that develop when belonging to a particular community, the traveler finds the Eternal Path of his or her journey to be the One that brings him or her Home.

Now the traveler sees and partakes of what was not previously available. This process is at the *Center of a Revelation* that speaks of *Being Created*, a priori, in a timeless continuum elsewhere, prior to engaging in *the Journey of Separation*, and revealing the true purpose of the fractional and temporal, existential experiences. The Creator's Light, bestowed as a Will-Full act and Pleasure on those Chosen ones, brings into existence Reality, and the accompanying understanding highlighting the meaning of Resurrection and Eternal Life.

For the uninitiated, suffering from the Principle of Separation, and living the Greatest Lie, this Realm does not exist. It is useless to make any reference to that condition of Oneness in the hope that something within will change and they will see, with the Spiritual Eye, a glimpse of the nature of that Reality and be forever changed.

They live in the land of error and ignorance, denial and falsehood, disputing even the miracle of an ordinary, physical life. Dead of the Spirit, their lives are blind imitations of their egoic desires, and will continue that way, time and again, throughout myriad cycles in worlds of time, names, and appearances that hide the Sun of Truth from mortal eyes.

The same goes for the sleepy souls, the traveling renegades whose hearts harbor the egoic traces of rebellion or disobedience. They, too, remain prisoners of desires, and passions, and the vanity reserved for the ignorant.

Pray to be resurrect and quickened, led unto *the Light of Guidance and Salvation* and lifted from a life of error and ignorance. Eons may have passed, but the opportunity comes again and again, slowly to rise from the dead and be counted as a believer and lover. Having received the Love of God, all travelers can now begin the Journeys of service.

Each traveling entity lives and experiences his or her own mind-world construct, while sharing the same plane of existence within the Simulator and Trainer. Each of these mind-world constructs reflects, by degrees, the Spiritual understanding of the voyage, reflecting, thus, the entity's own sphere of Soul-based awareness as a process of transformation and state of nearness with the Beloved of all these worlds.

All entities abide within a community, creation-wide, of eternal companionships, though many are unaware of this Reality, as they live an apparently separate existence within a local, planetary system of Life and Intelligence.

This conditional appearance of separation will be revealed as an illusion, part-and-parcel of the entity's transformation at some future time, a necessary artifice of a fractional and temporal, existential experience within the Simulator, with no other value outside that plane. Those that continue to progress in their transformative journeys will understand, little by little, as their veils of ignorance are removed by the intensity of the Light of nearness, as they approach the Truth that God does what He Wills and Please on whomever He chooses.

This process of Spiritual transformation is pre-ordained and pre-recorded, built-in with selected experiences as a means to an end. The objective of our existence is the complete understanding of one's True Self—who we each really are.

Imagine, then, living and experiencing this world of time and co-mingling with others whose mind-world constructs share many common experiences. We are thus able to communicate and coexist, interacting and building relationships, as friends and lovers, within the same world. The opposite is also true, those entities who are unable to communicate and share this plane of existence, who lack the ability to develop relationships as friends and lovers, live worlds apart.

Similarly, developing the transformative process, over a linear time, together or not, brings the staying ability or lack of it, to sustain harmony and remain together.

Within a complex environment where different roles are played, each favoring unique rituals and traditions, differing in language and geographical localities, cultural backgrounds and education, food and shelter, wealth and poverty, that differ also in up-bringing conditions of growth and change, constructive or destructive, a societal population is difficult to unite, and peaceful lives for its members a daunting challenge to accomplish.

In short, such are the worlds upon worlds within a planetary system of Life and Intelligence that are sharing on a continuing basis a physical plane of existence with built-in dimensional states, as individuals, Soul-based or not; Spiritually connected or not to the Universal System of Life and Intelligence; with a mind and body that is coherent and functional by degrees, or not.

To this scenario all we have to do is add the myriad planetary systems of Life and Intelligence within a

Galaxy, their complex interactions and relationships, omni-dimensionally present, and multi-directionally expanding, coupled to many other galactic systems of Life and Intelligence, integrated and slowly bringing to bear their own systems of Life and Intelligence, by degrees, into one Universal System, one of several, that represent, together, the _Creation of the God and Creator_ we are all cognizant of, or not, with a Divine Plan of Oneness of Being and Manifestation, for each and all of His creatures, being guided by His Manifestations, _His Divine Educators_, that cyclically come and go.

Their Delivery and Dispensation of the Divine Energetics, the Spiritual Information, to perform the Soul-based transformation and integration towards a Oneness of Being and Manifestation, is the Purpose of the Simulator and Trainer.

The _individual's sentient Spiritual Awakening_ becomes, then, the first step in the right direction, with many others to follow.

Orbs

Each mind-world construct—what each of us understands and feels—who we think we are and understand, becomes the source of either fulfillment and happiness or an emptiness by degrees that is reflected in many ways, from depression and agony, to unhappiness, anger, hatred, or simply boredom.

River of Love

When God's Love flows,
The heart's opening
Lets in the world—
One Soul at a time.

Joy

For every rainbow's
Tears of sadness,

God sends drops of joy
From His Ocean
Of Compassion.

The Wonder

Helplessness
Is the sign
Of God's help
Coming.

Who else can form
Spirals of galaxies
As easily as unfolding
Ferns, or open
The blue skies
With jagged bolts
Of power
And admonishing
Rumbling
Of His Voice?

One life's speck of time
Disappears in eternity—
Held

In the immensity
Of His embrace.

The patterns in one's lives should let each traveling entity know his or her conditional state of Being, and the process of becoming one's Higher Self lets us know how near or far from the Truth we each are—how close we are to following God's Will and Pleasure.

Finding the Point

Beyond the end of the trail
Lies the point of Return.
The journey
Cannot be measured
In time.
Lying within
The way an apple seed
Is encompassed
Within its inner star—
Waiting for the outer
Red and white covering
To be exposed to Light
By the sharp Word
Of Truth.

The *Principle of Separation* rules the process of Oneness of Being and Manifestation during the Journey. The farther away we are from the Soul's Knowingness, the greater the separation from the Truth and the Perfections within that Oneness. The traveler knows whether his or her Orb of Understanding is correct and complete, or not, by simple introspection upon the life experiences lived. Are we each being directed towards fulfillment and happiness, or towards an emptiness by degrees that is reflected in many ways, from depression and agony, to unhappiness, anger, hatred, or simply boredom?

The process of exploration and discovery has one simple guideline: in a paraphrase of Sun Bear, does your understanding produce corn to eat?

When the object and effect of the traveler's life to reflect the inner happiness and feeling of fulfillment and contentment is absent, it is time to revise what we think we know and understand. We are, after all, *stand-alone, bi-directional and non-linear, scalar carrier waves*, conditioned by the impositions (modulations) upon them from the environment and genes, our own egoic-selves, and from high above (or deep within), our Soul-based states of pure awareness.

If our conditioning from the time we are conceptualized within the womb lacks the proper information, or the information is erroneous, the traveler is exposed to the distortions that over time bring about an actuality (the way things are) far from the intended goal of the Creator.

The entity loses the ability to reflect inner perfections, the realization of the Oneness of Being that most often lies dormant in a world of time.

When entities interact within the same plane of reference, these discrepancies pulling them away from the desired goal of the Creator's Intelligent Design do not bring the desired results supporting coherence, consistency, unity, soundness, and common sense. An obvious lack of clarity ensues, charging interactions with frustration and anger, jealousy and envy, in a package that leads to conflict and eventual violence.

If we increase exponentially the number of interactions under these premises, war becomes the unnatural outcome. This special effect is meant to assist us in our exploration and discovery within the Simulator and Trainer—the workshop of temporal life—to conclude that something is not working.

When the channel to the Higher Self, one's True Identity, does not allow us to participate in full, the obvious sources of understanding and decisions are the modulations from the third and fourth dimensions— we simply become the actors (egoic-selves) in the *play of life*. Without the understanding of the higher rules of engagement—righteous actions and compassion, love and forgiveness, and one's submission and surrendering to the Will of the Creator—the possibility of a positive outcome is non-existent.

Behaving contrary to the (Divine) Intelligent Design cannot possibly bring the results intended by the Source. We were not created to act like the wild beasts of the field. We were created as divine entities able to express the melodies of a Paradise that lives within each one of us, a Paradise immersed in the Love of the Creator.

When our orbs of understanding do not bring the desired goals of the Creator, we cannot act as one, or be united by the individual, inner mechanism bringing the integration of a Soul-based point of view with the Spirit of Life and Intelligence of the Universe(s) (those imperceptible fields of activities acting as pre-cursor engines, fifth-dimensionally, to what is expressed in the theater of existence) through one's mind (a fourth-dimensional construct), and one's third-dimensional unit of travel (the body).

Sadly, by ignoring the rules within the Simulator and Trainer, all the travelers that are the deniers and the doubters, stuck within the pit-stops of the first and second stories, are delayed in becoming their Higher

Selves. They are thus unable to support the collective Spiritual Growth, with some individual exceptions.

As such, there is a _2094 Sanction_ determining a moment when this planetary system of Life and Intelligence cannot support life as we know it. This conscious collective consent reflects, without a doubt, the Divine assent of a Creator for the termination of a Program of Development no longer viable for the designed results. This has occurred before, and will continue to take place for as long as His creatures' wills run against His Will and Pleasure. There is no end to these cycles, processes that bring about sincerity and faithfulness. The Simulator and Trainer was designed with this goal in mind. This quasi-eternal system of Life and Intelligence sieves and separates _the wheat from the chaff,_ in a contrasting environment filled with special effects that demonstrate, clarify, and allow for corrections and changes. All entities are moving forward towards the intended perfections that lie within each traveler's Oneness of Being. At a certain point, as determined by the Creator, the creature and servant of God is able to Manifest and express, without distortions, those Perfections created by the Lord of all the worlds.

A New Perspective

An architect has an idea, and over time designs a house. The blue-prints are then used by a civil engineer who builds it. The house is later sold by a realtor. The new homeowner purchases it, and now lives within *that idea*.

That house sits in a community where other houses have gone through the same process, over time, many other travelers now live within those ideas. That community is part of a city, an expression of many ideas—thought-forms—from many sources, built by several engineers over time, with differing designs and usefulness. This city is now a reflection of those ideas, a much larger place that gathers the interactivity of the many travelers who live within it.

And so it happens with each state and nation. Ideas become reflected and become the material construct we all reside within and experience—from ideas that have been expressed over larger quanta of time.

This world is part of a larger construct, a galaxy, with its many planet-world communities, all generated from the ideas of their inhabitants, who are themselves residing within and experiencing those material constructs.

All of these galactic communities are a part of a larger ideation, reflected and made to be sense-perceived and experienced, a universe that is also an Intelligent Design of someone or something greater than any one of us. We don't call its Creator an architect or an engineer or both. We don't know what to call the Creator of it all, so we use simple words, like God or Dios, etc., depending on the language used. Better yet, we can all agree that it is best to call the Creator an *Unknowable Essence*—My creature is My Mystery, and I am his Mystery.

This *First Idea* that emerges from utter nothingness, the Creation we are all experiencing and are a part of, has to have a reason. The best reason is: The Creator wants to be known!

The most interesting thing is that this Creation, *a thought-form* that was expressed as a reflection of God's desire bringing the creature and everything else, into Being, *Because of a Known Love, I engraved Mine Image within thee and have revealed my Beauty thereof.*

And thus we all live eternally within His Creation. This Creation has *a Purpose*: for all entities to experience nearness to the Creator by being reflections of what lies hidden within each one of us, a Oneness of Being and Manifestation. It is this process, especially the latter part, the Oneness of Manifestation, that will not only express the content within the Oneness of Being, but also express His Kingdom as Desired and Willed. Through this reflected expression, the creature experiences his or her True Identity and higher Self, lives within the precinct of His Love and Protection, and enjoys True Freedom.

The entity's journey through myriad worlds of time is the process that allows for Remembering and Returning. All those experiences, as a cumulative packet, are looked at in retrospect. This act of going to the past, whether the past is a few minutes ago or many years, and contemplating upon those memories (and those recovered), as well as reflecting on their import, with as little egoic input as possible, is called, *Remembering and Returning*.

By Remembering, we Return to our Higher Selves. The reason for the necessity of this process is the difference between the Simulator's worlds of time and the Everlasting Realm's eternal now.

The two differing perspectives derived from these two different conditions cause a relative effect upon our experiences.

Linear time, with a future, an imaginary present far too short to be glimpsed, and a past, within worlds where time has a known beginning and a known end, fragments our experience of the eternal-present found in the Reality in which we all exist as our True Selves.

We were created in a Realm where time has no known beginning and no known end. We live and experience, within the Simulator and Trainer, worlds of time that have a known beginning (when you were born), and a known end (when you will die). To be able to correlate and reflect upon the import of our experiences, _we must look back into our past in acts of reflection_. We thereby become cognizant of their value as we understand the emerging patterns. We can then connect our personal lives and experiences with everything else—a whole universe of possibilities within each of us begging for exploration and discovery.

Integrated in Soul-based Awareness, Spirit of Life and Intelligence, and mind and body, the entity captures Information that is relevant and timely, dispensed for his or her journey of Remembrance and Return. This _Spiritual Transformation_ assists each traveler to fulfill his or her mission. Those experiences were, and are, pre-ordained and pre-recorded according to the Eternal Wisdom of a Creator whose handiwork, the entity and His Mystery, He guides to completion.

The Creator's work in an eternal time becomes an immediate reflection of His Will and Pleasure upon the entity. The entity, in turn, must reproduce, echo, and mirror what lies within his or her Oneness of Being (as created by God). This Beingness is a depository of His Trust in each one of us. It grants to each of His creatures a progressing practice, a means to the end of Spiritual transformation, the actuality (the way things are) of the experiences in a world of time. The entities' righteous actions then become replicated as a likeness of that initial Image of Perfection from a Higher Realm.

There is a caveat and note: the egoic-self must not alter, distort, restrict, resist, avoid, ignore, or act against said developmental opportunity with actions that will greatly delay the journey and process of Remembering and Returning.

The individual outcomes of this transformational process are omni-dimensional, and its patterns multi-directional. Each inner expression, within unique roles and scripts, cultures and traditions, follows a diversity of rituals, languages, environmental conditioning, belief systems, education and training, etc., skewed in one way or another, within its own bubble of understanding and feelings, grouped into balloon communities built-in with familiarities and objectives, alliances and agendas, beyond individual intents and attitudes. Those myriad distractions from the goal of Oneness stand as a reminder of how far from the mark the race has ventured, and how difficult it is to bring about a logical frame of reference and agreement.

Nothing short of a cyclical intervention, an adjustment and reminder to all travelers, can change the _self-destructive course_.

The Voice we hear, or no longer do, takes flesh and calls all travelers to reflect upon their inner beauty and Oneness of Being. Those hearing the call respond, and form a community readied for the transformation that follows—many are called; few are chosen.

Restoring the Heart

Love is a verb

Deep within the Soul's well
Lies the Mystery
Of God's Love.
It cannot be touched.
Instead it waits
Patiently for us
To wake up!
Suddenly it floods
The landscape
Of consciousness,
Turning the dry sands
To blossoming colors.
Everyone becomes
A friend of the Friend.

The cardinal on the branch
Sings more sweetly
In his just-pressed,
Red uniform.

If we could reach
Through the sky
And hold God's hand,
We would, at this moment,
Nod our heads in time
To the music
Of quick, cascading notes
And the slow
Revolution
Of Galaxies.

This *means to an end* begins with *the search* for the Beloved of all the worlds, the Manifestation of God for the day and age of the traveler's emergence unto the shores of consciousness in a world of time.

The *Seeker of the Truth* is responding to the *Clarion Call of the Beloved*, and unbeknown to him or her, the search has begun.

The desert of life has yet to offer the traveler the cup of water that soothes the thirst of the Spirit of

Life and Intelligence. The plains of heaven have yet to unfold the path that leads to the Beloved.

The wanderers of life move to-and-fro, looking everywhere for a sign. The seed of this stage is _patience_; yet they know not. Many lives will be spent. The downtrodden travelers will continue in the sojourns, despite it all.

Those that seek the Friend will be guided. Those that perceive the signs will have cleansed their hearts from any remnants and attractions that distract the Soul. The true seeker never gives up, no matter how difficult the challenges are.

And when illumined by the Love of the Traceless Friend, the seeker faces the Ocean of Love and melts away. Here pain addresses the life of the seeker, and without the pain of Love this sojourn would never end. Love here makes reasoning to vanish and the un-burning fire to shut the gates of hell forever as the Spirit becomes purified.

As one door closes and another opens, the traveler enters the goal of _Understanding_, the _Knowledge_ that will set him or her free from doubt in order to embrace certitude. Clarity dawns. The seeker knows that there is a purpose and direction to the madness found in the theater of life.

The seeker lives the experience of life, sighing with separation from the Beloved. Empty of heart, he or she approaches, not knowing whence to satisfy that hunger. Despairing and alone, driven by anguish, the traveler finds the Garden—and finally the light of Reunion. Had the traveler known beforehand that the peril and anguish would lead to the Light that illumines, that Being's countenance and attitude would have changed.

If the traveler knows of the communion and prayer experienced through the Holy Spirit, and, observes the mysteries of the Friend, he or she will walk straight into _Unity_ with the Beloved.

Here the Oneness of Manifestation is understood and sought. The illusion of the many names and appearances found in a world of time is torn by the Light of True Understanding. The seeker walks the talk, and is guided deeper within, with knowledge no longer confined in the prison of the egoic-self and passion.

Here the lover sees all the pathways of Love, and the many endeavors that will enable him or her to reach the Beloved. The seeker learns to leave behind the burdens of an illusory life.

From sorrow to happiness, as the illusions are rent asunder, the seeker comes to the life of the Spirit. At this stage there is only God. The traveler witnesses the beauty of the Friend. He or she finds the Mirror of the Soul in need of cleansing.

The seeker looks further within to discover that all the blessings may be received by the humble servant.

The seeker has been guided to that Holy Place where one's insignificance in relation to the Almighty is realized. From this state of Being the traveler faces the Beloved of all the worlds, standing at the gate of his or her heart.

The Journey within the Spiritual Heart, the seat of the Soul, begins.

Recognition and acceptance of He Whom God made Manifest is the Key and the standard of a Spiritual requirement to enter into the Planes of the Heart of the Beloved—the four stages that lead to one's True Self, a process that Restores the Heart of every creature traveling within the Simulator and Trainer.

The creature understands the need to surrender all the senses, the mind and the heart, to the overwhelming melody of Love and harmony of Wisdom.

The seeker will face the Perfect Mirror, attuned to the Songs of Revelation. There is no option except to go forward and face the experiences that cleanse the Soul.

The first of these four stages of the Heart reveal the purpose of Obedience and the Law of God. The Mirror of the Spirit as one's True Image surfaces, no longer obscured by the distortions of corruption and vain imaginings. The seeker struggles with his or her behavior and morality before acting. When this inner conflict is overcome, the traveler attains the *second stage* of facing the Higher Self.

Here, Righteousness and Compassion triumph, as the Image becomes more and more clear. The entity begins the process of surrendering his or her personal will to the Divine Will, until the inner Image of Beauty begins to shine outwardly.

Out of a deeper Love for the Beloved, the traveler seeks to unravel the mysteries of Remembrance and Return. The seeker now embraces with a pure heart and a clear mind the inner Oneness of Being reflected within. In the *third stage*, the Heart of the seeker of Truth opens, becoming truly and wholly reflected in the Mirror of the Soul. The Heart is restored—alive.

The travelers in these Planes of Limitation now live more fully their destined experiences in a world of time, each one cognizant of the purpose and significance of such an existence—where the Whole is found within. They now are experiencing the Return, as they Remember that everything begins and ends in God.

As the Assayer finds the seeker fit to advance to the fourth stage of the Heart, the Being of Light is plunged into the Plane of Oneness, uniting with _the Source_ of that pure Image and Reflection in the Mirror of the Soul. Oneness of Being has become Oneness of Manifestation. One's True Self is now realized, seeing and hearing with the Divine Eyes and Ears, in alignment with all life everywhere in all the worlds.

The Seeker lives and experiences _the Word_. There is no separation from the Source.

The New Language of Love

When the *Heart is Restored* and made like a newly-born babe, free from the encumbrances of all previous detrimental and injurious spiritual occurrences and their effects, the travelers through worlds of Life and Intelligence are made anew—knowing when they need to know

This re-birth means that the traveler is endowed with new Eyes and Ears to behave in accordance with the Divine Intelligent Design.

The traveler's understanding has shifted to his or her heavenly awareness with *the information* that redirects one's actions in strict conformity with *the rulings of an eternal domain*. These edicts or *pronouncements* protect each entity within his or her newly re-gained *original station* as a divine creature and servant of God.

The traveler's state of *Oneness of Being* must now be reflecting a *Oneness of Manifestation*. Nothing short of a clear and pure flow of the River of Life is permissible or tolerable at this stage of the Spiritual process enveloping the traveling entity within the Simulator and Trainer.

Constancy and sacrifice lead the traveler to a full surrender and submission, to acquire the certainty and tranquility afforded in his or her journey by the Ultimate Truth—He does what He Wills and Pleases, on whomever He chooses.

How the Love of God, now present in the Heart of the traveler, is reflected and echoed, redirected and exhibited in every-day life is at the foundation of the entity's state of happiness and contentment. The Love of God fulfills each entity's original Mission: one of complete integration and Oneness with His Creation. This process is exhibited through an emerging pattern in which an eternal signature is introduced into the temporal world and all its relationships, stamping a world of time with the birthmark of an eternal civilization.

Nothing short of the understanding of one's divine destiny, unencumbered by attachments to the illusions derived from a planet's fourth-dimensional, mind-world constructs, will suffice to sustain the goal of His Desire.

The Love of God must be retained and remain always in its pure state within the heart of the traveler. This deposited Trust represents the on-going connectivity necessary to Remember and Return to one's True Self. This active Trust must be never severed, or unacknowledged by the grateful recipient.

Among the many responsibilities to be acknowledged and rigorously followed, throughout all the relationships and interactions within the Simulator and Trainer, is the *Sacredness of Life*.

For the Love of God to coexist within each and all Hearts, the sacrosanct and inviolable principle that life should never be taken nor any Heart injured pre-supposes our acceptance of *a Principle or Primal Code*, from Source, sustaining the existence of the individual and civilization.

This Principle is the basis and determinant of the overall quality that rules the Heart of Creation. It is the Wellspring of harmony and tranquility, joy and fulfillment. When this Code or Principle lacks its full expression in the landscape and theater of existence, an individual, or a collective expression of that same Self-expression of life, loses its connectivity to the Soul, and to the Spirit of Life and Intelligence. The result is the type of civilization we are experiencing right now on Earth—a civilization full of suffering—physical, mental, emotional, and spiritual. This mayhem resulting from the manifesting of selfish or misguided desires was _never_ God's Plan for His Beloved creatures.

The intricate web of omni-dimensional and multi-directional interactions of the universe's Life and Intelligence knows no distinctions, nor does it discriminate among the choices and determinants for actions that lead in one or another direction—life is Life.

When it comes to the individual traveling entity, the same criterion is true and applicable. How well throughout his or her sojourn an entity follows the Primal Directive, the standard from which there is no acceptable deviation, may only be determined by the quality of Life that Being is experiencing. The _proof is in the pudding_.

One of the most shared, familiar, and repeated activities among all travelers, as an example, is found through the expression of one's feelings. The way we feel in a given moment becomes the source and foundation of all of our actions towards self and others.

The way we feel about anything or everything originates in the way we feel about ourselves. How we feel about ourselves is the by-product of a very important and critical relationship and interaction with our Creator. This interaction is also about Love!

Do we Love our Creator? Without this *initial act* of love for our Creator, His Love cannot reach us.

This precondition is a necessary Root-connectivity, our Soul-based state of pure awareness reaching out in gratefulness for our existence. This act from the creature to the Creator becomes the initial point of departure and reference, the Light guiding the vessel throughout the Journey, the signature and indicator of Eternal Life.

Anything disturbing this spiritual arrangement causes us to lose the spiritual compass and way during a sojourn in a world of time. It also, invariably, brings a re-occurring theme of returns to worlds of time. When the entity's attention on the Source is lost, that being descends to egoically-made conditions that bring to the forefront the absurdities that incarcerate the entity, with the attachments and addictions associated with pain, suffering, and anguish.

Of these several consequences, born out of bad habits, ill-feelings, and lack of information (not knowing), the patterns that recycle the most, time and again, have to do with the personal relationships between genders. Relationships meant to be the foundation of an eternal and ever-advancing civilization, built from eternal companionships nursed from the Love of God, have morphed into abominations and abhorrences against the Divine Plan of God.

Entities, most often in the role of males, desire sexually-derived pleasure that knows no boundaries. This excess is abusive and violent, even in the mildest expressions. Each Soul-based creature's gifted existence by the Creator was designed for goodness and moderation. Any behavior that runs contrary to this principle brings the negative results we observe as emotional, psychological, and bodily disturbances that render relationships dysfunctional, both individually and collectively.

We ask,

Can the Love of God exist in such hearts?

A civilization built upon such a fundamental condition will never know peace and tranquility, when at its core, the relationships between the genders is so out-of-balance. The great majority of men has yet to acknowledge women in a fair and just way.

For God's Love and Wisdom to prevail in a world of time, all entities, in whatever gender role, must honor equally all other entities. All must recognize the delicate gift of the Soul-based awareness and Spirit of Life and Intelligence of God's creatures.

There is an ongoing violation within the entities known as _human_, especially upon the female of the species. This intrusion and encroachment go beyond material rights, lack of respect, or even physical safety and health.

Relationships on Earth have been destroyed because there is an unconscionable _breach of the Trust of God_. The _eternal companionships_ that the Creator brought into existence in the beginning that has no beginning have been sliced apart by the sharp sword of deception—the addictive chemistry created hormonally by immoderate use of sex beyond its intended use of a single, procreative act agreed upon by a man and a woman who wish to have a child to make mention of God.

When physical sex is utilized in a way that defies and disobeys the Creator's Intent, that action interrupts the flow of His Love for His creature—whether that creature be in the role of a male or female.

When God's Love for His creature cannot fill the heart of that precious being, that entity becomes modulated by much lower influences—environmental as well as egoic. In this way, unfortunately, the beloved servant of God becomes lost. Instead of expressing his or her God-given _virtues_, the vacuum of that being's heart and susceptible mind becomes filled with what may be designated as _satanic_ influences—the negative emotions and thoughts of anger, greed, envy, and discontent leading to the expressions of crime, war, and abuse of all kinds.

Since killing, stealing, and hurting others are actions that we know violate God's Laws, we are certain that any actions of excesses that result in those negative conditions also violate God's Laws.

There is no excuse for treating another human being in a way that harms that extraordinary Being of Light.

An entity in the role of a man, for example, does not have the so-called _right_ over the use of another's body—be that the body of an entity in the role of a woman, a man, or even the body of an entity in the role of a boy or a girl.

For the face of violence and abuse does not end with the female of the species. Children, young adults, and, indeed, all ages and sexes are subject to these horrific anomalies created by _humans_ who act more violently towards their own species than most animals do towards theirs.

Furthermore, animals simply act from instinct, whereas those who are _supposed to act from the Soul-based point of view and the Spirit of Life and Intelligence_ are far more destructive than those creatures guided only by instinctive intelligence.

The unfortunate result of generations of abuse is that those children who were abused, grow up without knowing how to parent, and those wives who were abused by their husbands (including having sex demanded of them at any hour of the day or night), know not how to be loving and affectionate companions and mothers, even though they know in their hearts they were born to express themselves in that felicitous manner!

Instead of the God-given Eternal Companionship that a couple's relationship was meant to be, the couple finds itself in a constant struggle. Instead of the ever-flowing Ocean of God's Love sustaining a man and a woman's love, for example, a mish-mash of ill-feelings, created by constant resentments, occurs.

Anger and disdain for life, depression and lack of Self-worth, are neither normal nor necessary. They are simply a result of wrong actions, and, in the case of a marriage, most often the result of the overuse of physical sex, and the underuse of the natural expression of God's Infinite Love through gentle, compassionate touch and affection.

This type of affection, referred to in the authors' book _Restoring the Heart_, as the "_Room of Affection_," emphasizes the Heart's Knowingness of both individuals. As both Beings tune into their deepest Well of Love, flowing forth effortlessly from within the Soul, a new kind of connection occurs that lends itself not only to the gentle closeness of physical hugging, kissing, and caressing, but also to a merging of the Light Bodies of both servants of the Eternal One.

There is no separation among all entities at the Soul level. We simply reflect various colors and rays of Light from the crystal of the Soul as it shines this way and that.

This deep connection is only available to those who do not bring in the third-dimensional aspect of physical intercourse. As has been mentioned, the exception is those few times when both eternal companions _agree to conceive a child_ in order for that entity to integrate his or her Soul-based viewpoint with a physical form, so that this newly-incarnated entity may act as a servant of God.

One sacrifices a short period of physical sex for an eternity of Life with one's eternal companion: two Soul-possessing Light Beings carrying out God's Will and Pleasure for all His creatures everywhere.

The authors _are not_ advocating being nuns or monks within a relationship. Quite the opposite! This type of Love, that can only be experienced within an eternal companionship where the two people have been brought together by God, leads to the most refined and wonderful feelings through the sense of touch. Together with the blessings of the Creator, they create a symphony of Love that can only happen when God holds them both within His flowing, Infinite, and Mysteriously Immeasurable Awareness.

This Love is not new—only forgotten by most within the present civilization (Adamic Cycle). And yet, for this civilization to have any hope of being renewed and revived, human love superposed and transformed by God's Love must be welcomed and embraced by all.

Because of hormonal influences upon those entities in the role of the male human, it is particularly imperative for men to re-assess their ways of interacting within relationships, especially within the courtship, marriage, or family settings.

As we have shown, humanity is in urgent need of the experience of the Love of God and Its bonding properties in order to fix that which is broken in our human family.

Men on Earth—you can choose to be _Heroes_ by practicing God's Love in all your relationships. You can choose to place the imperative knowledge and wisdom coming straight from _your own Soul and Spirit_ *through your Heart* over the (most probably genetically-modified) chemical and hormonal influences that give more importance to a part of your body than to the Whole Divine Plan for Creation!

You, wonderful creation and creature of God, can do this.

You only have to ask God to help you. When you surrender your tiny will to His Will and Pleasure, there is no limit to the good that you can do on Earth.

Men, women, and all the beautiful creatures of One Creator, *can act according to the Divine Plan* and resuscitate the dying race of humanity.

The abuse and violence perpetrated against over half the world's population, mostly occurring behind closed doors, cannot continue.

The Heart of the Life and Intelligence of the Planet must be restored to bring the peace and tranquility needed to foster our very existence.

In Conclusion

What will it take for entities traveling through this heap of dust to understand the need for change? How may we become cognizant of the beautiful station destined for each of us? How may we know that we are incarcerated in a world of names and appearances, forming a world-construct that gives a mere temporal significance, a mirage or illusion, that begins to fade from the moment of our arrival?

Despite the facts faced and the enormity and gravity of an actuality that demonstrates, every day and every moment, how off-center and distorted our understanding of the Reality that should exist is; despite the fact that our Spiritual history gives credibility and weight to how lost we are within our Selves; we are still unwilling to throw in the towel.

After all, God has placed His Trust in our very Heart and Soul. _That_ cannot be ignored.

There is so much beauty found naturally in our environment, and brought into existence by the Self-aware artists that create. This magnificent orchestration as an expression of what lies within our planetary system of Life and Intelligence, when manifested amidst the horrors perpetrated by other members of the very same race, makes us wonder.

How can such an extreme contrast serve a purpose of educating and guiding the blind and dead of Spirit?

But it does!

Let's look at the situation on our planet logically for a moment.

That Love which is from God is Infinite, All-Powerful, and every other Divine Attribute. That Love which is chemically- or hormonally-based is temporary, fallible, and dependent upon an entropic physical system which will at least fail at the death of the body, and usually is only sustained for a far shorter time.

When *eternal* companions leave their physical bodies at death, their Love, based as it is in the Divine Gift and Love of God, continues with them.

When a married couple has based their love on the act of physical sex, even along with friendship, they will never have had a chance to develop that permanent, immortal bond in the same way.

What humanity requires is a new understanding of immortal Love—one which combines the aspects of Soul-based awareness, the Spirit of Life and Intelligence, harmony between the minds and the bodies of the two eternal companions, and a new expression of touch and affection whose *Intent* is *not* a fleeting, physical orgasm emphasizing the material realm, but rather the Unity and Oneness of both eternal companions with each other and with their Creator Who has bestowed upon them their immortal existence!

Although this experience is already known at the Soul and Spirit level as the basis of pure Love between eternal companions, most entities in human form have become addicted to the illusion of love based on physical, hormonal feedback and have thereby unwittingly destroyed the basis of happiness for both their companions and the rest of society.

Once the intent and attention of an entity has been directed away from the higher, infinitely-knowing and loving aspect of his or her Self towards the confused, and often manipulated, material, mental, and emotional aspect of Being, the *other* person in a relationship automatically becomes *an object for one's own pleasure*.

If, instead, the two eternal companions surrender their egos, ask to be filled with His infinite Love, receive that Love, and then share that Love through loving and affectionate touch, they may be forever blessed.

This Connection, rooted within God's intent for His precious creatures, allows each companion to experience at least a taste of the paradisiacal Kingdom, as it transforms and uplifts our experiences of this seeming world upon Earth.

Those that question the validity of this latter experience have neglected to fulfilling, within them-Selves, the pre-requisites of purity of Heart, and clarity of mind. Since all traveling entities that arrive into a planetary system of Life and Intelligence find themselves, sooner or later, encapsulated and held like prisoners by their degree of understanding and related feelings—where they are meant to be always—it is of no use to argue or explain that others' personal experiences, of a different nature and derived from a different Spiritual view point, are not imaginary, but Real.

The seeker that was guided to the understanding of the ultimate Truth, that the Creator's Will and Pleasure rules over whomever He chooses, knows that such an experience is by invitation only. Following, and joined to that realization, comes the opening of a mystical portal revealing aspects of a more Advanced Realm that remains inaccessible—veiled—to those entities that have yet to be transformed spiritually. This transformative process is one of the objectives of the fractional, and temporal, existential experience.

It is important to understand the difference between intellectually understanding something, anything, and actually experiencing it first-hand. The experiential experience, in the case of the spiritual transformative process, is individually earmarked, that is, selected exclusively, for that individual, and varies in content and results based on many factors, including his or her sincerity and faithfulness.

We remind all travelers to endeavor to complete each experience as mandated by the All-Knowing One.

When the _Oneness of Being_, as created, becomes expressed as a _Realm of Oneness of Manifestation_, as desired, His Will becomes the creature's will, and His Love is then the way the creature feels.

Salutations, and God-speed.

Books by Kito and Ling Productions

For Adults:
www.loginthesoul.com

Echoes of a Vision of Paradise, If You Cannot Remember, You Will Return, Volume 1

Echoes of a Vision of Paradise, If You Cannot Remember, You Will Return, Volume 2

Echoes of a Vision of Paradise, If You Cannot Remember, You Will Return, Volume 3

Echoes of a Vision of Paradise, If You Cannot Remember, You Will Return, a Synopsis (Also available as Audio Book)

Restoring the Heart

The Simulator, A dream within a Dream

The 2094 Sanction

A Being of Light, God's Will and Pleasure

Paradise, The Science of the Love of God

Experiences and Insights

The Key

Modulation on the Stand-Alone Scalar Carrier Wave, Freedom or Incarceration

Oneness of Being and Manifestation, Beyond the Dream: The Anchor Point

For Children:
www.loginthesoul.com

Titles and Brief Descriptions

Andy Ant and Beatrice Bee (With a Bonus Coloring Section)

Beauty is on the Inside (With a Bonus Coloring Section)

Bee and Fairy Power (Super-fairies, Bees, and Organic Farmers team up to save Nature and Humanity)

Fly, Fly, Louie Louie (A Story of Change and Identity. With a Bonus Coloring Section)

Grandma and I / Mi Abuelita y Yo (A Bilingual English/Spanish Story, with a Bonus Coloring and Drawing Section)

How Alexander the Gnome Found the Sun (With a Bonus Coloring Section)

Igor's Walkabout (With a Bonus Coloring Section)

Katie Caterpillar Finds Her Song (With a Bonus Coloring Section; also available as Audio Book)

Return to Paradise (Happy the Bluebird and Bright-Wings the Cardinal use Virtues to restore the Professor's Home)

Saving Lantern's Waterfall (An Eco-Adventure)

The King and the Castle (Love Flies in on the Wings of Destiny. With a Bonus Coloring Section)

The Language of Love: Twelve Bilingual Plays Teaching Virtues, for Children to Perform (Accompanying Book for Return to Paradise)

Printed in the United States
By Bookmasters